INSTANT GROUP DEVOTIONS for Children's Ministry

Group
Loveland, Colorado

INSTANT GROUP DEVOTIONS FOR CHILDREN'S MINISTRY

Copyright © 1998 Group Publishing, Inc.

Credits

Contributing Authors: Debbie Gowensmith, Jim Hawley, Karl Leuthauser, Julie Meiklejohn,
    Janis Sampson, Amy Simpson, Beth Rowland Wolf, and Paul Woods
Acquisitions Editor: Jan Kershner
Editor: Candace McMahan
Chief Creative Officer: Joani Schultz
Copy Editor: Janis Sampson
Designer and Art Director: Jean Bruns
Cover Art Director: Jeff A. Storm
Computer Graphic Artist: Joyce Douglas
Cover Illustrator: Michael Morris
Illustrator: Stacey Lamb
Production Manager: Peggy Naylor

Unless otherwise noted, Scriptures taken from the HOLY BIBLE, NEW INTERNATIONAL VERSION®. Copyright © 1973, 1978, 1984 by International Bible Society. Used by permission of Zondervan Publishing House. All rights reserved.

Library of Congress Cataloging-in-Publication Data

Instant group devotions for children's ministry.
        p.   cm.
    Includes index.
    ISBN 0-7644-2043-7 (alk. paper)
    1. Children--Prayer-books and devotions--English. 2. Church work
  with children. I. Group Publishing.
BV4571.2.I57   1998
242' .62--dc21   97-43837
                                         CIP

10 9 8 7 6 5 4 3 2   07 06 05 04 03 02 01 00 99

Printed in the United States of America.

Visit our Web site: www.grouppublishing.com

Contents

Instant Devotions About Families

Instant Devotions About School

Instant Devotions About Friends

Instant Devotions About Faith

Instant Devotions for Special Days

Introduction

Welcome to *Instant Group Devotions for Children's Ministry!* Here are fifty-four new devotions that speak to some of the key issues kids face within their families, with their friends, at school, in their faith, and on special days from New Year's Day through Christmas. And they do it in fun, interactive ways that involve kids' five senses and appeal to a variety of learning styles.

Use these devotions for children's sermons, Sunday school, junior church, after-school programs, vacation Bible school, day camp, and any other settings in which children are gathered. All of the activities may be adapted to fit your group's size. If you have a small group, do the devotional activities together. If your group is larger, divide into small groups.

Be creative, and have a great time leading your children into deeper walks with God with *Instant Group Devotions for Children's Ministry.*

If you are looking for more resources that offer active, easy-to-prepare, and simple-to-lead devotions that help children understand and apply God's Word to their daily lives, try *Quick Group Devotions for Children's Ministry* and *Fun Group Devotions for Children's Ministry,* both from Group Publishing.

INSTANT DEVOTIONS ABOUT

ABOUT

Families

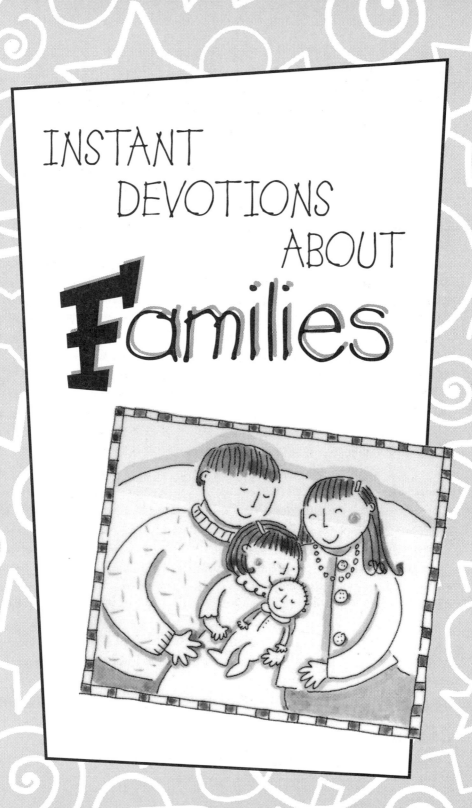

Reach Out and Help

THEME: Kindness

SCRIPTURE: Luke 8:40-42, 49-56

OVERVIEW: Children will play Reach-Out Tag and relate this game to a Bible story about Jairus' family.

PREPARATION: You'll need Bibles and an open space for Tag.

Experience

Tell children they're going to play Reach-Out Tag. Select one child to be "It" and another child to be chased. Have remaining children hold hands in pairs and scatter over the playing area. Ask pairs to stay in place once the game gets underway. Tell children that the one being chased will be safe if he or she can grab a pair's hand. When a person's hand is grabbed, the two become a new pair and the other child of the pair must run from "It." If "It" tags the person, that person becomes "It," and the game continues. Ask pairs to reach out as far as they can to help the person being chased. Allow kids to play Reach-Out Tag a few minutes, then have them form trios and sit down.

Response

As kids get settled in their trios, give each trio a Bible, then say: **This game reminds me of a story in the Bible about how Jesus reached out to help a family. He helped the dad, the mom, and their little girl. Let me read this story to you from Luke 8. You can follow along.** Read aloud Luke 8:40-42 and 49-56.

Say: **Discuss the following questions in your trios. When your trio finishes responding to each question, reach out your hand, palm up, if you want to share one of the answers with the whole group.** Ask:

- **In what ways does Jesus reach out to help the father in this story?**
- **In what ways does Jesus reach out to help the little girl?**
- **In what ways does Jesus reach out to help the mother in this story?**
- **Can we reach out to help members of our own families the way Jesus did? In what ways?**
- **Can we help other families, too? In what ways?**

Closing

Say: **It's true! We can help our families and other families, too. And I think you can help each other right now.** Ask kids to form a tightly knit circle and sit down. Then say: **After the prayer, when I say "amen," show me that you can stand up together shoulder to shoulder without using your hands. Ready?** Pray: **Help us, Jesus, to get up and reach out in love to our families and others. Amen!** Applaud kids' united effort to stand up and reach out.

uild Them Up

THEME: Encouraging others
SCRIPTURE: 1 Thessalonians 5:11
OVERVIEW: Children will practice building each other up.
PREPARATION: You'll need a Bible, tape, a sheet of newsprint, and colorful markers.

Experience

Tape the newsprint to a wall. Then draw a small stick person in the center of the sheet of newsprint. Point to the stick person and say: **This is my friend Sam Nobody. He's been feeling pretty bad lately—he's been feeling as if he can't do anything right. Let's see if we can encourage him. Think of encouraging things to say to him. You might think of encouraging words others have told you, or you might think of encouraging words you wish others would say to you.**

Have children take turns saying encouraging words to Sam Nobody. As they say their words, have them use a colored marker to draw a person-shaped outline around the stick person (see illustration). Continue for several minutes until the children run out of encouraging words or until you run out of room on the newsprint.

Response

Say: **Look at Sam Nobody now. He sure looks like a somebody, doesn't he?** Ask:
- **What's different about Sam now?**
- **How did encouraging Sam make you feel?**

- **If Sam were a real person, how do you think he'd feel now?**

Say: **There are lots of people like Sam in the world—pretty special people who feel low and discouraged. These people feel small and insignificant. But the Bible tells us how we can help them. As I read this verse, I want you to listen for two things. First, listen for what we can do to help people like Sam. Second, listen for the word picture that tells us what will happen to people like Sam when we follow the advice in this verse.**

Read aloud 1 Thessalonians 5:11. Ask:

- **What can we do to help people like Sam?**
- **What was the second thing the verse mentioned—the word picture that tells what will happen to people like Sam when we encourage them?**

Say: **When we encourage people, we're building them up. Look at how small Sam felt at the beginning. See how strong he looks now. That's what happens when we encourage others—we make them feel better and stronger.**

Closing

Say: **There are people all around us who need encouragement. I want you to think of three people you can encourage—a family member, a friend, and someone at school or church who you don't know very well. Find a partner, and tell him or her how you'll encourage these people this week.**

Give children a few minutes to find and talk with a partner.

Pray: **God, we want to be encouragers. We want to help build up each other. Help us be encouragers in everything we do this week. Amen.**

Bubbling Words

THEME: Cheerfulness

SCRIPTURE: Proverbs 17:22

OVERVIEW: Children will add sugar to glasses of cola, causing the cola to overflow. They'll compare the experience to the effect of cheerful hearts and words.

PREPARATION: You'll need a Bible and enough cola to serve your group. You'll also need a cup of sugar, spoons, disposable cups, paper plates, and paper towels.

Experience

Give each child a paper cup on a paper plate. Have paper towels nearby. Fill each cup half full with cola. Say: **This cola is sweet and cold and good. But before you drink it, let's try an experiment.** Ask:

● **What do you think will happen if we add sugar to the cola?**

Don't comment on the probability of children's predictions. Instead say: **Let's add the sugar and see if your predictions are right.**

Have each child add a teaspoon of sugar to his or her cup of cola and stir. The cola will bubble up.

Response

When the bubbling has stopped, ask:

● **What effect did the sugar have on the cola?**

Read aloud Proverbs 17:22, then ask:

● **How can you relate what happened with the cola to having a cheerful heart toward your family? with your friends?**

● **How does a cheerful heart affect others?**

● **What do cheerful hearts do for those who have them?**

Say: **I know we would all agree that life is much more pleasant when we have cheerful hearts and use cheerful words instead of grumbling words. Cheerful hearts help us to express our love, appreciation, and respect for others. Let's practice using cheerful words.**

Closing

Have children sip their cola drinks. Some may request cola without the additional sugar. As children sip, have them share cheerful words they could share with their families. Then pray: **God, you've given us families to love and encourage. We want to show your love to them. Help us do that by offering cheerful words from cheerful hearts that cause your love to bubble up and run over in our lives. Amen.**

The Gift of Obedience

THEME: Love
SCRIPTURE: Ephesians 6:1-3
OVERVIEW: Children will make special pictures and their own wrapping paper and learn about the gift of obedience.
PREPARATION: You'll need a Bible. Gather together newsprint; small boxes; small pieces of paper; transparent tape; and various craft supplies such as washable markers, crayons, stickers, and rubber stamps.

Experience

Make the craft supplies available to the children. Give each child a small box and a piece of newsprint large enough to cover the box. Say: **We're going to make our very own wrapping paper for some very special gifts.**

Instruct each child to use the craft supplies to make the newsprint into a piece of wrapping paper. Encourage children to make unique and beautiful wrapping paper creations. When children have finished decorating the newsprint, give each child a small piece of paper. Instruct children to draw pictures on the small pieces of paper. Tell them their pictures are special gifts for their parents. When the pictures are finished, have children place the pictures inside their small boxes.

Show children how to use their wrapping paper to wrap their small boxes. You may want to provide extra touches such as ribbons and bows and to encourage the children to decorate their boxes with them.

Response

When children have finished wrapping their boxes, ask:
- **What do you think of the gift you've made?**
- **How do you feel when you give someone a beautiful gift?**
- **Why do you think it can be so fun to give gifts to others?**

Read Ephesians 6:1-3 aloud. Then say: **God says we should obey our parents. When you obey your parents, you give them a wonderful gift. Parents love to receive the gift of obedience.** Ask:
- **How is obedience like giving your parents a gift?**

Closing

Encourage children to show their gift-wrapped boxes to one another. As they do, ask them to name ways they can give the gift of obedience to their parents.

Ask them to talk about specific new ways they will obey their parents during the upcoming week.

When each child has had a chance to share, close in prayer. Encourage children to take their boxes home and give them to their parents.

1 Instructions of Love

THEME: Honoring your parents
SCRIPTURE: Proverbs 6:20-22
OVERVIEW: Children will create reminders of important instructions to help them appreciate their parents' instructions.
PREPARATION: You'll need a Bible, crayons or markers, fifteen-inch lengths of yarn, and construction paper hearts. Before class, use a hole punch to create a hole in the top of each heart.

Experience

Gather kids around you, and say: **Let's pretend it's very cold and windy outside and that the corner** (designate a corner of the room) **is "outside." OK, everyone, let's go outside.** Go to the corner with the kids, and say: **It's very cold and windy out here! Let's pretend that we didn't wear our coats and hats outside. We're cold!** Encourage kids to hug themselves, shiver, and sneeze. Then say: **Uh-oh, it's starting to rain, so we'd better go back inside.**

After leaving the corner, gather kids around you and ask:

● **What's it like to be in cold weather without a coat and hat?**

● **Why do you think someone would instruct you to put on a coat and hat before you go outside in cold, windy weather?**

● **What are some other instructions people tell you to help you?**

Then say: **Think of an instruction that could help your friends in some way. It could be one of the instructions we just shared, or you can think of a new instruction.** Give kids a few seconds to think of instructions, then say: **We're going to make special reminders to help our friends remember our instructions.** Have kids write or draw their instructions on the construction paper hearts. Then

Teacher Tip

Be sensitive to the fact that some children aren't raised by their parents. If you wish, you can change the language of this devotion to include all caretakers instead of just moms and dads.

13

show kids how to string a heart on a piece of yarn and tie the ends of the yarn to make a necklace.

Response

After everyone has made a necklace, gather kids around you, and read aloud Proverbs 6:20-22. Ask:

● **Why do you think our parents give us instructions?**

● **How are the instructions we thought of like the instructions our parents give us?**

● **What do you think the Bible means when it says, "When you walk, they will guide you; when you sleep, they will watch over you; when you awake, they will speak to you"?**

● **What are some benefits of remembering what our parents teach us?**

Teacher Tip

If the subject of parents' imperfection arises during the discussion, talk about it with the kids. Remind kids that all people need God's help—even parents. Explain that parents make mistakes and need their kids' forgiveness just as kids make mistakes and need their parents' forgiveness. Focus the discussion on the fact that God loves each of the kids and their parents and wants family members to love each other. Make yourself or another adult available to your kids if they want to talk privately about problems they're having with their parents.

Be aware of your legal responsibilities if a child indicates that he or she has been abused. Some states' laws require adults to report suspicions of abuse; check with the child-protection agency in your state to learn more about your legal responsibilities.

● **What might happen if we don't remember what our parents teach us?**

● **How are the necklaces we made as reminders like fastening our parents' instructions around our necks?**

Say: **When our parents give us instructions, they're usually trying to help us. They're trying to keep us from getting sick or hurt, or they're trying to help us do well. When we remember the good instructions they give us, our lives are better.**

Closing

Have kids form pairs. Say: **When you made your necklace, you thought of an instruction that would help your friends. Tell your partner your instruction, and explain how that instruction can help your partner.** Pause while kids share. Then to help kids remember the instructions they learned, have partners exchange necklaces.

Close with a prayer, asking God to help the kids use the good instructions from their parents to live good lives.

low-Motion Speech

THEME: Communication/listening

SCRIPTURE: James 1:19

OVERVIEW: Children will do a slow-motion relay and discuss how being "slow to speak" will help in their communication skills.

PREPARATION: You'll need Bibles, lightweight paper plates, a chalkboard and chalk, markers, and scissors. Before class, use masking tape to designate the finish line for a relay.

Experience

Have kids form two teams and line up single file opposite the finish line. Give the first person in each line a paper plate, and ask the person to balance the plate on his or her head.

Say: **This is a relay race. You must race to the line at the opposite end of the room with a plate balanced on your head. If the plate falls off your head, you must start over.**

After kids have run the relay, have them each pair up with someone from the other relay team, and give each pair a Bible.

Teacher Tip

If there are more than twelve kids in your class, form three or more teams. If the teams are unequal in number, join the team with fewer members.

Response

Ask:

● **How was this relay different from others you've run?**

● **What did you have to do to succeed?**

● **When is it a good idea to do something slowly?**

Have one person in each pair read James 1:19, then have the other person summarize the verse in his or her own words.

Ask:

● **Why do you think it is good to be slow to speak?**

Say: **Just as it was easier to balance the plate if you moved slowly, it's easier to listen to others if you're slow to speak. Think of situations in which it's hard to be "slow to speak." It might be when you're angry with a member of your family or a friend.**

Give kids a minute to think of situations, then ask kids to share their responses with their partners.

Closing

Have kids form groups of four, then give each group one of the paper plates used in the relay, a pair of scissors, and four markers. Have kids cut the paper plates into fourths. Write James 1:19 on a chalkboard, and have kids write the verse on their paper plate pieces.

Close with a prayer that reiterates James 1:19: **Lord, help us all to be quick to listen, slow to speak, and slow to become angry. In Jesus' name, amen.**

Encourage kids to place their paper plate reminders where they will see them often.

Being Helpful Brings Unity

THEME: Unity
SCRIPTURE: Psalm 133:1
OVERVIEW: Children will help each other complete a task they can't do by themselves and discuss the importance of family unity.
PREPARATION: You'll need a Bible. For each person, you'll need a ten-inch piece of string or yarn, construction paper, pencils, and scissors.

Experience

Give kids each a piece of string, and ask them to tie it around their wrists. Allow kids about a minute to attempt this. Ask:

- **Why are you having a hard time tying the string around your wrist?**
- **What could you do to make it easier?**

After kids have offered suggestions, tell them to find a partner. When kids have paired up, suggest they find a solution to their problem within their pairs.

Response

After kids have discovered that the solution is to do the job for their partners, ask:

- **Was it possible to tie the string on your wrist by yourself? Why or why not?**

Read Psalm 133:1 aloud. Ask:

● **How did having your partner help you tie the string on your wrist make you feel?**

● **Who can tell me what "unity" means?**

● **How did this activity show unity?**

Have kids form groups of four. Say: **Tell your group about a time you helped someone in your family and what happened because of it.**

Closing

Using construction paper and pencils, have kids outline their hands.

Say: **In this activity, you used your hands to help each other. Think about how you could use your hands to help someone in your family.**

On the hand outlines, have kids each write one thing they will do to help bring unity to their families. Then give kids scissors and allow them to cut out the hand outlines.

Close in prayer, asking God to help the children bring unity to their families.

Encourage kids to take their hand cutouts home as reminders of their commitment to family unity.

Care Cards

THEME: Generosity

SCRIPTURE: Matthew 6:2-4

OVERVIEW: Children will learn about generosity by creating gift cards for secret pals.

PREPARATION: You'll need a Bible. You'll also need one piece of construction paper for each child and plain paper. Gather a variety of art and decorating supplies such as markers, glue sticks, glitter glue, pasta, chenille wires, tape, and tissue paper. Before class, write each child's name on a slip of paper.

Experience

Ask:

● **Have you ever done something really nice for someone else? What happened?**

● **Would you rather do kind things for someone else or have kind things done for you?**

Say: **Each of you is going to do something generous for someone else in this room right now. I'm going to give you a slip of paper with the name of your secret pal on it. Don't let anyone know who your secret pal is.**

Give each child one of the slips of paper you prepared and one sheet of construction paper. Make certain all the students have a secret pal. As kids look at their slips of paper, set out the decorating supplies.

Say: **We're going to make secret cards for our secret pals. Begin by folding your sheet of construction paper in half. Write your secret pal's name on the front of the card, but don't let anyone see it. Then use the supplies I've set out to make a card for your secret pal. Show your appreciation and God's love for your secret pal in the card. But don't put your name on it. Remember— it's a secret.**

As kids work, make certain that they have written the correct names on the front of the cards and that no one has been overlooked.

After about five minutes, gather the cards, and set them in a pile in the middle of the room. Have children each go through the pile to find the card addressed to them.

Teacher Tip

If you are doing this activity with younger kids, whisper the name of the secret pal to each child.

Teacher Tip

If kids aren't certain what kinds of messages to write on the cards, you can suggest writing "God loves you more than life" or drawing hearts and smiley faces.

Response

Ask:

● **How did it feel to get a card from your secret pal?**
● **How did it feel to make a card for your secret pal?**
● **Which did you like more?**

Have a volunteer read Matthew 6:2-4 aloud. Ask:

● **Why should we do kind things for others?**
● **Why do you think Jesus wants us to keep our giving a secret?**
● **Should we be generous toward others even when we know they won't thank us? Why or why not?**
● **How do you think God will bless us for the generous things we do?**

Say: **It's fun to do kind things for other people. We enjoy making others smile and making them feel good. Jesus wants us to be generous for the right reasons. If we do good things for others so they'll like us, we're probably**

18

doing them for the wrong reason. **If we do generous things for others to make them feel good and to show God's love to them, we're doing them for the right reasons. That's why doing kind things in secret is such a special thing.**

Closing

Have kids form pairs, and give each pair a sheet of paper and a pencil. Instruct pairs to list all the generous things they can do for members of their families. After a few minutes, have each student choose one thing on the list that he or she would like to do right away. Encourage kids to do the things in secret as soon as they get home.

Close by praying: **God, thank you for all the generous things you've done for us. Please help us do kind things for others—whether they find out about them or not. In Jesus' name, amen.**

Many Parts, One Whole

THEME: Cooperation/working together
SCRIPTURE: I Corinthians 12:27
OVERVIEW: Children will work together building imaginary "machines" and learn how to cooperate with others.
PREPARATION: You'll need a Bible.

Experience

Have kids form groups of four and say: **I'd like you to make imaginary machines in your groups, using your bodies as the machine parts. Each person in a group will act as one working part. Some of the things machine parts might do are turn around in circles, jump up and down, and jog in place. Start by having one person in your group act like a machine part, and then have each person add his or her part to the machine one at a time. When you've created your machine, be prepared to explain what it is and demonstrate how it works to the whole group.**

After groups have finished demonstrating their machines, have members of each group present their

Teacher Tip

If you have a smaller group, the whole group can make one big machine.

machine to the whole class as they explain what their machine is and how it works.

Response

After all of the presentations, have kids sit in a large circle. Ask:

● **How was each person in your group an important part of your machine?**

● **If one person's part had been missing, would your machine have worked as well? Explain.**

Say: **The Bible shows us that every person has an important place in the work of God.** Read 1 Corinthians 12:27 aloud, and ask:

● **What do you think it means to be a part of the body of Christ?**

● **What gifts and talents do you think you bring to the body of Christ?**

● **What gifts and talents do you think the members of your family bring to the body of Christ?**

● **How can we help each other use those gifts and talents to the best of our abilities?**

Closing

Have kids form pairs and share with each other what gifts and talents each partner adds to the body of Christ. Ask a volunteer to close in prayer before dismissing the group.

Obeying Parents, Obeying God

THEME: Obedience
SCRIPTURE: I John 5:3
OVERVIEW: Children will experience obedience and examine how loving God means obeying him as well as obeying parents.
PREPARATION: You'll need a Bible. For each child, gather a lightweight object such as a chalk eraser, a booklet, a small toy, or a plastic bowl.

Experience

Give each child a lightweight object, and say: **Stand up, place your object on your head, and turn around in a complete circle. You may hold your object on your head if you need to.**

After kids have done that, say: **Now stick your right elbow out to your side with your hand on your chest. Place your object on your elbow, and turn around again.**

Collect the objects, and have kids sit down. Then ask:

● **Did any of you feel a little silly doing these things?**

● **How often do you do silly things?**

● **Why did you do what I told you to do?**

Say: **We usually do what people tell us to do if we love and respect those people.** Ask:

● **Who should we love and respect most of all?**

● **How can we show God how much we love him?**

Say: **The Bible says that if we really love God, we'll obey him.** Have a child read aloud 1 John 5:3. Then ask:

● **Does God tell us to do silly things like putting something on our heads and turning in circles? Why or why not?**

Have kids form groups of three or four to answer the following question:

● **What kinds of things does God want us to do?**

Allow kids to discuss the question for about a minute, then have them report their answers to the rest of the group. Say: **One thing God wants us to do is to obey our parents. When we obey our parents and do what's right, we're obeying God.**

Closing

Say: **No one is perfect at obeying God or parents. All of us can do better. Think right now about one thing you can do to obey God and your parents better.**

Allow volunteers to share things they can do to obey better. Then say: **In a minute I'm going to pray. When I pray, I'd like you to pray silently, asking God to help you obey your parents better than ever before.**

Close the activity with prayer, asking God to help kids obey their parents as they seek to obey him, too.

School Authorities

THEME: Authority
SCRIPTURE: Romans 13:1
OVERVIEW: Kids will experience being under authority and examine the idea that God puts others in authority over them.
PREPARATION: You'll need a Bible and one penny per child.

Experience

Have kids form pairs. Say: **The person in your pair who's closest to me is going to be the Teller, and the person farthest away will be the Doer. Teller, you'll tell your partner something to do; and, Doer, you'll do it. For example, a Teller might tell his or her partner to cluck like a chicken, and the Doer will cluck like a chicken!**

Teacher Tip
If you are outside of the United States, substitute a coin from your nation in this activity.

Once everyone understands the instructions, say "go." Give kids a minute to tell and do, and then have partners exchange roles so that each child has a chance to play each role. Ask:

● **What was it like to be the Teller?**
● **What was it like to be the Doer?**
● **How was being a Doer in this activity similar to being told what to do in life?**

Say: **People often tell you what to do. Sometimes other kids tell you to do bad things, but usually people tell you to do good things. God wants us to obey the people who tell us to do the right things.**

Response

Ask:
● **Who can tell me what authority is?**

Give kids a chance to respond, and thank them for their answers. Then say: **In a way, authority is the right to tell someone what to do**.

Ask:
● **Who has authority over you at home?**

- Who has authority over you in our city?
- Who has authority over you at school?
- What do you think the Bible says about obeying authorities?

Have someone read aloud Romans 13:1. Say: **God put people in author-ity over us for our own good. They can help us learn and keep us safe. Sometimes it's hard to obey authorities, just as it's hard to always do what the teacher says at school.**

Ask:

- How can teachers and other authorities help us and keep us safe at school?
- What sometimes makes it hard to obey a teacher at school?

Say: **Even when we don't feel like it, God wants us to obey the author-ities he's put over us. And we can know that God is always in control, even when we don't like the authorities who are over us.**

Closing

Give each child a penny. Ask:

- Whose picture is on the penny?

Say: **Abraham Lincoln was president of the United States. He was a man God put in authority over the country. Every time you see a penny, think of the peo-ple God has put in authority over you and remember to obey them.**

Wrap up the devotion by asking God to help kids remember to obey authorities at school and in every part of their lives.

Teacher Tip
If there are kids younger than four in your group, do not give them pennies because they can be choking hazards.

Working Together?

THEME: Competition
SCRIPTURE: James 3:16-18
OVERVIEW: Children will participate in a role-play that shows the effects of competition.
PREPARATION: You'll need Bibles and photocopies of the "Working Together?" handout (p. 27). Cut apart the sections of the handout. You'll need one handout for every group of four children.

Experience

Have children form groups of four. In each group give a different section of the "Working Together?" handout (p. 27) to each child, but don't let kids know what roles the other children in their group have. After children have read their roles, give them five minutes to play their parts.

After five minutes, call time and gather children for a discussion. Have them sit in their groups.

Response

Ask:

● **What decision did your teacher make? How are you going to spend your day?**

● **Tell me what happened in your group. What emotions did you experience as you tried to persuade the teacher and as you competed with your classmates?**

Read aloud James 3:16. Ask:

● **Does this Scripture passage accurately describe what happened in your group? in what ways?**

Say: **In your group go around the circle and share other areas in which competition surfaces in your school. Then answer this question: What are the consequences and the effects of competition?**

Give children two or three minutes for their discussions. Give each group a Bible, and have someone read aloud James 3:16-18 in each group. Say: **Now discuss in your group what you can do to avoid the negative consequences of competition and act with the wisdom that's described in this passage.** Have children discuss in their groups and then share their ideas with the rest of the class.

Closing

Pray aloud: **God, we thank you for the opportunity to work and study with others. But we know that when we compete, sometimes our selfish desires get in the way of friendships. Sometimes we forget to think about others, and we think only of ourselves. Instead of competing, help us to work with each other in a way that is considerate and kind. Amen.**

Working Together?

Photocopy and cut apart this handout.
You'll need one complete handout for every four children.

ROLE 1: It's time to decide where your class will go on a field trip. You're a top-notch swimmer—the best swimmer in your class, in fact. You want to go to the water park. Persuade the teacher to take the class to Splash Land.

ROLE 2: It's time to decide where your class will go for its annual field trip. You've spent all your spare time studying the stars and planets—you know more about astronomy than anyone in your class. Persuade your teacher to take the class to the planetarium.

ROLE 3: It's time to decide where your class will go for its annual field trip. You're a great painter—the best artist in your class. In fact, you've spent the last three summers at art camp. Persuade the teacher to take the class to the Paint-Your-Own-Pottery store and to the art museum.

ROLE 4: You're the teacher, and you have to decide where to take the class for its annual field trip. Listen to the suggestions of your students, then decide where to go.

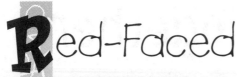

Red-Faced

THEME: Embarrassment
SCRIPTURE: Romans 8:38-39
OVERVIEW: Children will anonymously share an embarrassing moment and realize that nothing is so bad that it will separate them from God's love.
PREPARATION: You'll need Bibles, index cards, and pencils. Think of an embarrassing situation that you've experienced and that you'd be willing to share with the group.

Experience

Say: **There's something about each one of you that I know for absolute certain. I know for a fact that every single person in this room has been embarrassed at some time. And most of you have been so embarrassed that you wanted the ground to open up and swallow you! Let me tell you about something embarrassing that happened to me once.**

Tell your story, then say: **Because we're all good friends, we can talk about the embarrassing things that have happened to us without being embarrassed again. Think about something embarrassing that's happened to you, and write it down on one of these cards.**

Give each child an index card and a pencil. Have them each write an embarrassing event that has happened to them. Be sure to tell them that the cards will be read aloud so the incidents they describe shouldn't be so humiliating that they don't want to share them. Also tell them not to include names or anything else that would identify them to the rest of the group.

Give children a few minutes to write their ideas. As you gather the cards, glance over them to make sure you can read them. Ask kids to explain words you can't decipher. Then shuffle the cards, and read them aloud.

Teacher Tip

It might be a good idea to explain the difference between laughing as a means of ridicule and laughing because something's funny. You might say something like this: "We're good friends, and we want the best for each other. When we laugh at these embarrassing moments, we aren't laughing out of a desire to make fun of each other. Instead, we're laughing because embarrassing moments are funny and because we all realize that these things could happen to us."

Response

Say: **Isn't it good to know that everyone does silly things and that every-one feels embarrassed sometimes? Let's talk about embarrassment.** Ask:

- **Why do we experience embarrassment?**
- **What is it like to be embarrassed? Describe what happens to you and how you feel when you are embarrassed.**
- **Is embarrassment something that makes you feel closer to others or more isolated from them? Explain.**

Say: **Embarrassment makes us feel as if we stick out—as if others are looking at us and laughing. We're afraid that people will reject us because of the silly things we do. But everyone does embarrassing things. We all have bodies that sometimes do things we'd rather they didn't do. And we all say things that make us look foolish. But even if we did the most embar-rassing thing in the world, God would still love us. Listen to this verse.**

Read Romans 8:38-39 aloud. Ask:

- **How could this verse change how you feel about your embarrassing moments?**

Closing

Give children new index cards and Bibles. Have them write out Romans 8:39, inserting "nor embarrassing acts" right before "nor anything else in all cre-ation." Also have them change the word "us" to the word "me." Then pray, thanking God for always loving us, even when we do embarrassing things.

Weight Off My Shoulders

THEME: Anxiety
SCRIPTURE: I Peter 5:7
OVERVIEW: Children will drag a heavy blanket or sleeping bag, then compare that to the burden of anxiety.
PREPARATION: You'll need a Bible and a heavy blanket or a heavy sleeping bag.

Experience

Have children form two single-file lines, one on each side of the room, facing each other. Give the child at the front of one line a heavy blanket. Instruct that child to put the blanket around his or her shoulders and drag it across the room to the person at the front of the other line. The next child will then put the blanket around his or her shoulders and drag it to the child at the front of the line across the room. After handing off the blanket, ask each child to sit down and watch the other children.

Response

When each child has had a turn, ask:

● **What was it like to drag the blanket across the room?**

● **How would this activity have been different if you hadn't been dragging the blanket?**

Have a volunteer read 1 Peter 5:7 aloud, then ask:

● **How was the game we played like living with anxieties?**

● **How was it like giving your anxieties to God and letting him carry them?**

● **What are some things that cause you anxiety?**

● **What does it mean to "cast all your anxiety on him"?**

Closing

Have each child find a partner and tell that person about one burden that is causing him or her anxiety. Then encourage partners to pray for each other, asking Jesus to help them give their burdens to him.

Learning to Learn

THEME: Homework

SCRIPTURE: Proverbs 4:10-13

OVERVIEW: Children will discover information about their grandparents and learn why homework is important.

PREPARATION: You'll need a Bible. Plan to do this devotion in a setting where at least one parent of each child in your group will be nearby. Or get the information kids will seek in the devotion from parents in advance and have it ready to give to children.

Experience

After children assemble, ask:

● **Does anyone here know where your grandparents lived when they were children?**

Allow a few responses, then say: **We're going to learn right now where your grandparents lived when they were children.**

If possible, send children to a parent to find out. If not, group older kids with younger kids, and have them read the information you gathered in advance.

After four or five minutes, gather kids and have them report what they learned. Then ask:

● **What was it like to learn new information about your grandparents?**

● **How was this like doing homework?**

● **How was it different?**

Say: **Sometimes doing homework can be a real pain! But homework has a purpose, and that purpose is to help us learn. Let's take a look at what the Bible says about learning.**

Response

Have someone read Proverbs 4:10-13 aloud. Then ask:

● **What does this passage say about the importance of learning?**

● **How can it help us in our lives?**

Have kids form groups of three or four to discuss the following questions.

● **What does homework have to do with learning?**

● **How can homework help us in our lives?**

After a couple of minutes of discussion, have kids report what they've discussed. If kids tend to be frivolous about the discussion, ask other kids if that's what learning is all about.

Say: **Homework helps us learn. Sometimes doing things several times helps us remember them better. And then we'll really know what we need to know. For example, it helps to us know math when a cashier gives us change at a store so we can be sure we receive the correct change.** Ask:

● **What other times might learning things through homework help us in our lives?**

Closing

Ask:

● **What did you learn today about someone else's grandparents?**

Say: **That's one of the neat things about learning. Sometimes we can share it with others. And sometimes we can learn together by doing homework or projects with a friend.**

Have kids form pairs and share with each other what they learned in this devotion. Then have each partner share with the group what his or her partner learned.

Say: **You didn't actually do homework today, but you did learn. God wants us to always be learning because learning will help us in whatever we do.**

Pray a prayer similar to this one to end your devotion: **God, thank you for giving us opportunities to learn. Help us do our best and learn all we can so that we will honor you. In Jesus' name, amen.**

 an't Hide Cheating!

BEST for Upper-Elementary Kids

THEME: Cheating
SCRIPTURE: Hebrews 4:13
OVERVIEW: Kids will privately explore their feelings about cheating and the fact that God knows their hearts.
PREPARATION: You'll need a Bible and newsprint and a marker or a chalkboard and chalk. Cut out three large circles of red, yellow, and green construction paper to simulate a traffic light. Photocopy one "Cheater's Highway" handout (p. 34) for each person.

Experience

Place the traffic-light circles several feet apart from each other in a line (red, yellow, green) on the floor. Give each person a "Cheater's Highway" handout (p. 34); then form two groups, the Blues and the Purples. Say: **Each of you has a list of questions. On your own decide how you will answer** the questions. **Answer with one of these three traffic lights.** Point to the circles on the floor. **Go, or green, means yes; caution, or yellow, means you're not sure; and stop, or red, means no. To answer each question, move to the red, yellow, or green circle. The Blues should answer the questions in the order they are listed on the handout (from one to four). The Purples should answer the questions backward (from four to one).**

Mix up the kids so no one knows who is in which group. Say: **After you've answered each question by stepping on one of the circles, gather in a circle around me. Ready? Go.**

After kids have gathered around you, ask:

● **What did you learn about how you feel about cheating in this activity?**

● **Did any of your answers surprise you? Explain.**

Response

Say: **Each of you answered the questions without anyone else knowing how you truly felt about cheating. You may be tempted to cheat because you don't think anyone will find out.**

Read Hebrews 4:13 aloud and ask:

● **Would any of your answers about cheating change, knowing that God knows what you're thinking? Explain.**

● **Who is hurt when a person cheats? Why?**

● **How do you think God feels about cheating?**

Closing

Have kids again gather into the Blue and Purple groups to brainstorm answers to this question:

● **How can God help you resist cheating?**

Have kids share their ideas, and write the responses on newsprint. Mention several responses in a closing prayer while asking God to help kids the next time they're tempted to cheat.

Cheater's Highway

1. You studied for a test and know the answers. But a family emergency the night before causes you to blank out when the test is put in front of you. You see your friend's answers on his test. Do you cheat?

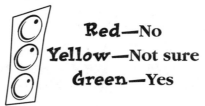

Red—No
Yellow—Not sure
Green—Yes

2. One teacher doesn't change tests from year to year. Your best friend gives you a copy of the test that he got from his older sister. The test has only the questions, not the answers. Will you take the test?

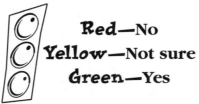

Red—No
Yellow—Not sure
Green—Yes

3. A popular person who you want to be friends with is looking at your test answers. She notices that you see what she's doing. Do you let her continue to look?

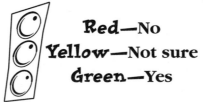

Red—No
Yellow—Not sure
Green—Yes

4. You and a friend are doing homework together. You don't understand a math problem, so you write down his answer on your paper. Is this cheating?

Red—No
Yellow—Not sure
Green—Yes

Doing My Best

THEME: Grades
SCRIPTURE: Luke 21:1-4
OVERVIEW: Kids will try their best in a progressively difficult game and compare that to doing their best in different school subjects.
PREPARATION: You'll need a Bible, three sheets of paper for each person, pencils, and a clean wastebasket. Write the letters A, B, and C on separate sheets of paper.

Experience

Place the wastebasket at one end of the room. Have kids form three groups: 1, 2, and 3. Give each person three sheets of paper, and tell kids to crumple the paper into balls. Place paper A about six feet from the basket, and have group 1 gather around the A. Place paper C on the other side of the room about twenty feet away (or as far away from the basket as possible), and have group 3 gather around the C. Place paper B in between A and C, and have group 2 gather around it. Make sure that everyone in each group has a clear line of fire toward the basket (see illustration).

Say: **Each of the paper balls you're holding represents a school subject. Think about three of your subjects. Think of one you do well in, one you do OK in, and one you struggle with. Each group is standing around a letter. If your group is standing around the A, the paper ball you'll toss represents your easiest subject; if you're standing around the** 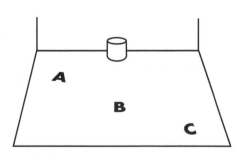 **B, the paper ball you'll toss represents your OK subject; and if you're next to the C, the paper ball you'll toss represents your hardest subject. When I say "go," each person is to try to toss only one paper ball into the basket. Ready? Go!**

After everyone has made one attempt, rotate groups as follows: group 1 to letter C, group 2 to letter A, and group 3 to letter B. Remind kids to think about what subject their paper ball represents according to the letter they're next to.

On your signal, have kids repeat the activity, using the second paper ball. Have kids rotate a final time: group 1 to letter B, group 2 to letter C, and group 3 to letter A. Have kids repeat the toss with the last paper ball. Ask:

● **When you tried to make a basket, which letter was easiest to be next to? hardest?**

Response

Read Luke 21:1-4 aloud, and say: **The widow gave Jesus a very small amount of money, but he praised her because she gave all she had.**

Ask groups to discuss:

● **How was the widow's effort and the effort you put into this game similar? different?**

● **Making a basket was probably harder the farther away you were from it. How is this like the subjects you struggle with?**

● **How can you give your best effort, especially in the subjects you struggle with in school?**

Say: **Some of you may do better than others in certain school subjects, and this may be reflected in your grades. But the important thing to remember is that Jesus praised the widow's *effort,* and he will praise your effort when you do your best.**

Closing

Say: **The paper balls you tried to toss into the basket represented your school subjects. When I say "go," pick up three paper balls, then gather in a circle. Go!** Pass out pencils, and have kids uncrumple the paper balls. Say: **Write the letter A on one sheet, B on another, and C on the third. Remember what subjects your three paper balls represented during our game? Write those subjects on your papers, then write one way you can do your best in each of those subjects.**

Close in prayer, asking God to help kids do their best in school.

Workin' for the Lord

THEME: Doing your best
SCRIPTURE: Ephesians 6:7-8 (New Century Version)
OVERVIEW: Kids will act out tough situations they may face and discuss how they can always "work for the Lord."
PREPARATION: You'll need a Bible, slips of paper, and pencils or pens.

Experience

Begin by reading Ephesians 6:7-8 aloud to the group, then ask:

● **What does it mean to always work as if you were serving the Lord?**

● **How would working for the Lord help you to always do your best?**

Have kids form pairs, and give each pair three slips of paper and pencils. Say: **I'd like you to brainstorm together in your pairs to come up with three tough situations you may face in your lives. Some examples are having to take a difficult test you didn't study for or having a fight with your brother or sister. Write one situation on each slip of paper. After you're finished, I'd like you to trade your slips of paper with another pair.**

Teacher Tip

If you have an uneven number of pairs, have pairs stand in a circle and have each pair pass its slips of paper to the pair on its right.

After pairs have traded situations, say: **Now I'd like you to take a few minutes to prepare three short skits in which you'll act out each situation. You'll need to end each skit by showing what a person would do in that situation if he or she were working for the Lord.**

Allow a few minutes for pairs to prepare their skits, and then have pairs perform for the class. Encourage kids to applaud each other's efforts.

Response

Have kids sit in a circle, and say: **I'd like each of you to think of one way you'll try to work for the Lord this week.** Go around the circle and have each person share what he or she is committed to do in the upcoming week.

Closing

Say: **Let's pray. Dear God, please be with us this week as we work to serve you. Help us to always remember to work for you. In Jesus' name, amen.**

Mission Accomplished!

THEME: Goals
SCRIPTURE: 1 Corinthians 16:13-14
OVERVIEW: Kids will complete an increasingly difficult sequence of actions and compare the experience to achieving goals they've set for themselves.
PREPARATION: You'll need Bibles.

Experience

Have kids stand in a large circle, and say: **We're going to talk about setting and achieving goals. The group's goal right now is to complete a sequence of actions that each person will add something to. The trick will be to remember the entire sequence.** Start off the sequence by performing a simple action such as clapping your hands three times. Have the person on your left add an action, and then have the whole group complete the sequence. Continue in this manner until each person has added an action to the sequence. (If your group is small, have each person add two actions to the sequence.)

When the entire sequence has been created, have kids complete it twice in a row, as fast as they can. Encourage kids to help and encourage each other.

Response

When the group has achieved its goal, have kids form pairs. Have pairs read 1 Corinthians 16:13-14 together and discuss the following questions. Then ask pairs to report their answers to the whole group.

● **What does this passage tell us about setting and achieving goals?**

● **How could this passage have helped us while we were completing our action sequence?**

● **What does this passage tell us about helping others achieve their goals?**

● **How did we help others while we were completing the action sequence?**

● **How can you use what we've discussed when you're setting goals?**

Teacher Tip
If kids have a tough time completing the action sequence accurately, use this as a teachable moment to discuss how we sometimes set goals for ourselves that are impossible to reach, then discuss what kids can do in those situations.

Closing

Have each partner think of one goal he or she has and share it with his or her partner. Have partners say a short prayer together to commit their goals to God.

Paper Toys

THEME: Boredom

SCRIPTURE: Ephesians 5:15-16

OVERVIEW: Children will create excitement from sheets of notebook paper.

PREPARATION: You'll need Bibles and a stack of notebook paper. Create one paper football as a model. Use a one- to three-inch-wide strip of paper and follow the directions in the "Paper Football" diagram.

Experience

Say: **I have a very special toy for each of you. The possibilities for using this toy are endless, and if you use this toy properly, you'll never be bored again. Are you ready to receive your toy?**

Give each child a sheet of notebook paper. Ask:

● **How do you like your toy?**

● **What don't you like about your toy?**

● **Do you think this toy is boring? Why or why not?**

Say: **At first glance a sheet of paper doesn't seem like a very fun toy. But it isn't the toys we have or the situations we're in that allow us to have fun— it's our own creativity. Let me show you what I mean.**

Have kids form four groups. Give each group a stack of paper. Say: **With your group use the paper I've given you to make an object that can be used in a fun and exciting way.**

As kids begin to work, offer suggestions to each group. Here are a few ideas to get you started.

Paper airplanes—Encourage kids to create a game or a contest using the planes.

Creative shapes—Challenge the group to develop a contest or a game that requires creative shapes made from paper.

Paper building blocks—Kids can stack flat sheets of paper on top of folded or rolled sheets of paper. Challenge kids to think of a creative game such as building the widest or highest building using the paper building blocks.

Paper footballs—Show kids how to "kick" field goals (see the diagram below), then challenge them to make a game using the footballs.

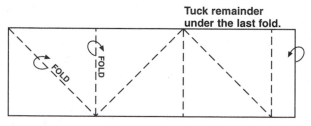

Response

After about five minutes, give each group a Bible, and have groups discuss the following questions:

● **Did you find a way to have fun with a blank sheet of paper? Explain.**

● **Before this activity, did you think a sheet of paper could be a cure for boredom?**

● **What did this activity teach you about boredom?**

● **With your group read Ephesians 5:15-16. How does verse 16 apply to boredom?**

● **What is one way you can make a boring class more interesting?**

● **What is one way you can avoid being bored at home?**

Say: **There really isn't any reason for Christians to be bored. In Ephesians 5:16 Paul encourages us to take every chance we have for doing good. We can always take time to talk to God or to serve others when we're bored. Boring times are really opportunities for us to do good things.**

Closing

Have kids form pairs and share the most boring thing they think they'll face in the upcoming week. Have kids pray that God will help them make the best of the experience by finding a way to do good and to show God's love in that situation.

INSTANT DEVOTIONS ABOUT Friends

A Special Treat

THEME: Forgiving others
SCRIPTURE: Matthew 18:21-35
OVERVIEW: Kids will receive treats and have the opportunity to share them in order to learn about forgiving others.
PREPARATION: You'll need Bibles. You'll also need enough bite-sized candy bars for each child to have two, or you may provide other treats of your choice.

Experience

Have kids form pairs, and make certain each pair has a Bible. Give one child in each pair two treats. Tell kids that they can begin eating their treats if they'd like to.

Have pairs discuss the following questions:

● **How did it feel to get two treats?**

● **How did it feel not to get a treat?**

● **What could you or your partner have done to make certain you both received a treat?**

Say: **Now look up Matthew 18:21-35, and read it with your partner.** After kids finish reading the passage, have pairs discuss these questions:

● **Why does God want us to forgive others?**

● **In what ways has God forgiven you?**

● **How are the treats in our devotion like forgiveness in the story? How are they different?**

Say: **If you shared one of your treats with your partner, you were doing what Jesus taught in Matthew 18:21-35. If you didn't share a treat, it's not too late. All of the people who were given treats—whether they shared them or not—can come to me and receive two more treats. You can take this gift and share it with your partner.**

Response

Have pairs discuss:

● **In what way is forgiveness a gift from God?**

● **How can we share the gift of forgiveness with others?**

● **Why should we share the gift of forgiveness with others?**

Closing

Have kids move as far away from each other as the room allows.

Say: **I'd like you to think of someone you're angry at. Take some time right now to forgive that person. Ask God to help you forgive the person and not to be angry at him or her anymore. Finish by asking God to give you a chance to be friends with the person again.**

Teacher Tip

If you have time, consider taking your kids through the following five-step process to teach them *how* to forgive others.

1. Ask God to help you forgive the person. Forgiveness isn't saying what the person did was OK—it's giving up your right to get back at the person or to continue being angry at the person.

2. Think of the exact thing the person did to make you angry—not, for example, "My sister is a jerk," but rather, "My sister hit me." Then say a prayer in which you forgive the person for the specific act: "I forgive my sister for hitting me," for example.

3. If you *can't* forgive the person, start all over again. It may take a long time, but keep trying until it happens.

4. Pray for the person. Ask God to help and bless him or her.

5. Try to become friends again—if it's safe. Forgiveness doesn't ever mean you should put yourself in danger or that you should keep letting yourself get hurt. But forgiveness does mean that you should try your best to get along with the person who hurt you.

Strength Bombardment

THEME: Self-identity/self-worth

SCRIPTURE: Psalm 8

OVERVIEW: Kids will learn how special they are to God and then "bombard" each other with strengths and positive qualities.

PREPARATION: You'll need a Bible and newsprint and a marker or a chalkboard and chalk.

Experience

Read Psalm 8 aloud, then say: **This psalm is a song of praise to God, thanking God for all of his wonderful creations. The psalmist is thanking God especially for creating his gifts to us.** Ask:

- **According to this psalm, how do you think God feels about humans?**
- **Why do you think people are so special and important to God?**

Say: **I'd like you to brainstorm the qualities that make people special. These could be qualities such as honesty, the ability to forgive, and generosity.** As kids call out their ideas, write the qualities on newsprint.

Have kids form groups of five or six. Say: **In your groups, I'd like you to stand up one at a time. When one person stands up, the other members of the group will "bombard" him or her by naming the strengths they see in that person's life. Use the list for ideas, and make sure each person in your group tells at least one strength of the person standing up. When the members of a group are finished bombarding the person standing up, he or she can choose the next person to be bombarded.**

Teacher Tip

Circulate among groups to help kids name each other's strengths. Remind kids to stay positive—no put-downs allowed!

Have groups continue in this manner until each person has been bombarded.

Response

Have kids form a circle and sit down. Ask:

- **How did this experience make you feel?**
- **How did this experience make you feel about God?**
- **How do you think God feels about you?**

Closing

As kids remain seated in a circle, have each person say a sentence prayer thanking God for the special qualities of the person on his or her left.

Tough Stuff

THEME: Sharing

SCRIPTURE: Luke 6:38a

OVERVIEW: Children will share fun things about themselves and then relate giving and receiving to friendship.

PREPARATION: You'll need a Bible, pencils, and index cards. You'll also need to have a trash can nearby.

Experience

Give kids pencils and index cards, then have kids form a circle. Say: **You look like interesting people to me. I want each of you to write on your card one interesting fact about yourself. Maybe you have a funny nickname or a goldfish named Blubber or you visited your cousin in Timbuktu.**

Give kids a minute or two to think and write, and then have them each pass their cards to the student on their right. Ask volunteers to read aloud any interesting facts written on the cards they've just been given.

Then say: **Now I want you to write on the card your favorite food—that is, what you think your favorite food would be if you lived on the planet Mars.** Give kids a moment to think and write, then have them each return their cards to the person on their left. Ask kids to share the fun responses.

Say: **It's fun to get together with friends, share with them, and find out what they're thinking. We give them information and receive information from them. Sometimes, though, we hurt each other, and then it's hard to talk about fun stuff.**

Have you ever done anything to a friend that you're ashamed of? Write down one word about what you did. For example, if you told a friend a lie, write down "lie." Or if you stayed mad at a friend, write down "mad." Or if you talked about friends behind their backs, write down "talked." Give kids a minute to write down their confessions.

Then say: **This time don't pass your card to someone else in the circle. Instead, think about telling God how sorry you are that you hurt your friend.** Pause. **Ask God to help you do the right thing.** Pause. **Now tear your card into tiny pieces, and throw the pieces into this trash can.**

Response

When the card pieces are all in the trash, ask kids the following questions:

- **What did you give when you passed your card to your neighbor?**
- **What did you receive from your neighbor?**
- **Were you worried about passing the card with what you had done wrong written on it? Why or why not?**
- **When someone says to you, "I'm sorry," what should you give the person in return?**

Closing

Say: **It's not easy to admit we're wrong, and it's not easy to forgive either. But after we do, we can move on to having fun and sharing good times together.** Read Luke 6:38a aloud, then close in prayer.

The Good and the Bad

THEME: Setting a good example
SCRIPTURE: 1 Timothy 4:12
OVERVIEW: Children will make lists of the people who've set examples for them.
PREPARATION: You'll need a Bible, paper, and pencils.

Experience

Distribute paper and pencils to children. Say: **Today we're going to talk about people who've set an example for us. I'd like you to take two minutes to write down a list of five famous people who've set a good example for you.**

Give kids a couple of minutes to complete their lists. Then have volunteers read their lists aloud. Ask:

- **Why do you look up to these people?**
- **What characteristics do these people have in common?**
- **What effect have these people had on your life?**

Say: **Now I have another request. Write down your personal top-five list of famous people who've set a bad example for you. Write only the** names of famous people—no teachers, friends, or family members.

After kids complete their lists, have volunteers read their lists aloud. Ask:

- **Why have you included these people on your list?**
- **What characteristics do these people have in common?**
- **What effect have these people had on your life?**

Response

Say: **Something I've noticed about people is that everyone sets some kind of example for others. We've talked about the examples set by famous people. But if you think about it, there are people all around us who do things that we admire. We want to develop some characteristic that they have. There are also people in our lives who have traits that we don't want to have, and we learn from their bad examples. Listen to what the Bible says about this.** Read aloud 1 Timothy 4:12. Ask:

- **What does this verse say to you?**
- **How can you be an example to others?**

Closing

Say: **You may not have realized that you're an example to other people. You can decide what kind of example you'll be. Take a few minutes to write down your own top-five list of ways you can be a good example to others.**

Give children a few minutes to complete their lists, then pray: **God, we know that you have called us to be examples of your love to the whole world. Thank you for those people who teach us by their good examples, and help us to develop characteristics that help us set good examples. Amen.**

Powers of Persuasion

THEME: Peer pressure
SCRIPTURE: 2 Corinthians 11:3-4
OVERVIEW: Children will play the game If You Love Me, Honey, Smile and compare it to the persuasive powers of peer pressure.
PREPARATION: You'll need a Bible.

Experience

Have children sit in a circle with about a foot of space between each of them. Choose a volunteer to be Honey. Honey must keep a straight face throughout his or her turn. One by one, choose other volunteers, or Persuaders, to say, "If you love me, Honey, smile." The Persuaders will use their persuasive powers to try to get Honey to smile. The Persuaders can make goofy faces, they can tickle themselves, and they can come within one foot of Honey, but they can't touch Honey or say anything except, "If you love me, Honey, smile."

If Honey smiles, the Persuader becomes the new Honey. If after a minute of "persuasion," Honey still hasn't smiled, choose another Persuader.

Response

Say: **Let's compare this experience to peer pressure.** Ask:

● **How was this game like or unlike peer pressure?**

● **What kinds of things are kids your age pressured to take part in?**

Let's read about a kind of peer pressure in the Bible. Read aloud 2 Corinthians 11:3. Ask:

● **What happened to Eve?**

● **What does this verse say might happen to us if we are persuaded by peer pressure?**

Say: **Listen again to 2 Corinthians 11:3. This time I'll read verse 4, too. While I read, think about how you can use the information in this passage to answer these questions:**

● **What are the warning signs of peer pressure?**

● **What can you do to keep yourself safe from peer pressure?**

Read the verses again, and then discuss the questions.

Closing

Say: **You've all had great ideas on how to protect yourselves from the bad influences of peer pressure. But there is a kind of good peer pressure. Good peer pressure happens when we encourage each other to live for God. Let's encourage each other now.**

To close, have children exchange high fives and say, "Live for Jesus" to each other.

The Wrong Ingredient

THEME: Gossip

SCRIPTURE: Proverbs 16:28b

OVERVIEW: Kids will make two recipes of lemonade, one with vinegar, and then compare the vinegar to gossip in a friendship.

PREPARATION: You'll need a Bible for the devotion. Before class, make one photocopy of "Lemonade Recipe 1" (p. 50) for every five students and one photocopy of "Lemonade Recipe 2" (p. 50) for every five students. Provide water; lemon juice; sugar; ice cubes; vinegar; small paper cups; and the following supplies for each group of five students: a pitcher, a stirring spoon, and measuring cups and spoons.

Experience

Have kids form groups of five. Give half of the groups "Lemonade Recipe 1"; give the rest of the groups "Lemonade Recipe 2." Provide ingredients, pitchers, stirring spoons, and measuring cups and spoons. Have each group follow its recipe to make a pitcher of lemonade.

When groups have finished making lemonade, give each person a small paper cup, and instruct each group to serve its lemonade to another group. When half the groups begin to complain about the bitter taste of the lemonade, allow them to dispose of the lemonade and refill their cups with the good lemonade.

Response

While students are drinking their lemonade, ask:

● **Why did some of the lemonade taste bitter?**

● **What was it like to taste that bitter lemonade? to serve it?**

Read Proverbs 16:28b aloud, then say: **Just as one simple ingredient ruined the lemonade recipe, gossip is an ingredient that will ruin a friendship.** Ask:

● **What happens when you add gossip to a friendship?**

● **Why do you think gossip makes people bitter?**

● **How is being talked about like drinking bitter lemonade?**

● **How is gossip like bitter lemonade?**

Closing

Allow each person to fill another cup with good lemonade and present it to someone else. As they present the lemonade to each other, instruct kids to say, "Just as I offer this gift to you, I'll offer positive words as gifts to my friends." Allow students to enjoy their lemonade, then close in prayer. Ask God to help kids resist the temptation to gossip and to keep their commitments to give their friends the gift of positive words.

Lemonade Recipe 1

8 cups water
2 cups lemon juice
1⅓ cups sugar
Ice cubes

Combine water, lemon juice, and sugar. Stir until the sugar is dissolved. Serve over ice cubes in paper cups.

Lemonade Recipe 2

2 cups water
2 cups vinegar
1 cup lemon juice
⅔ cup sugar
Ice cubes

Combine water, vinegar, lemon juice, and sugar. Stir until the sugar is dissolved. Serve over ice cubes in paper cups.

Sour Words

THEME: Hurtful words
SCRIPTURE: Proverbs 15:1
OVERVIEW: Children will chew sour gum then sweet gum, and talk about the way hurtful words make people feel.
PREPARATION: You'll need sour gum balls, such as Tear Jerkers, and sweet gum balls.

Experience

Give each child a sour gum ball. Encourage kids to chew their gum (if they can), then ask:

● **What do you think of the gum I gave you?**

Then give each child a normal, sweet gum ball, and allow kids to chew that gum.

Response

While kids are chewing their gum, ask:

● **What's the difference between the two pieces of gum I gave you?**

● **Which gum did you enjoy more? Why?**

Read Proverbs 15:1 aloud and ask:

● **How were the two gum balls like the words we can say to other people?**

● **How are the results of our kind words different from the results of our mean words?**

● **How do you feel when people say kind words to you? How do others feel when you say kind words to them?**

Closing

Have kids form pairs. Assign one person in each pair to be person 1 and the other to be person 2. Say: **Now we're going to see how using different kinds of words makes us feel and how hearing different kinds of words makes others feel. I will read about two different people, and you will respond in kind ways or harsh ways.**

If you're person 1, use kind words in this situation. If you're person 2, use harsh words.

A new boy has just joined your class. He's very quiet, but when he

does talk, he sounds really funny. Almost all the kids make fun of him, and he begins to cry. **If you are person 1, say kind words to the new student.** Wait a minute, so that everybody has a chance to speak. Say: **If you're person 2, say harsh words to the new student.** Wait another minute for kids to role-play.

Say: **Let's play one more. This time, if you're person 1, you'll respond with harsh words. If you're person 2, you'll respond with kind words.**

A girl was walking up the front steps at school, and she tripped and fell down. All her books and papers fell on the ground. Nobody has helped her, and school is about to start. Person 1, how will you respond to this girl? Give children about a minute to speak. Then say: **Person 2, now it's your turn to respond to this girl.**

Gather the group, and discuss the following questions:
● **How did saying harsh words make you feel? Why?**
● **How did saying kind words make you feel? Why?**
● **How do harsh words make others feel?**
● **How do kind words make others feel?**

Say: **It always feels better to give and receive kind words. Let's gather in a circle and say a kind word about the person on our right.**

Blind Judgment

THEME: Judging others
SCRIPTURE: Matthew 7:1-5
OVERVIEW: Children will experience seeing others through "imperfect" eyes.
PREPARATION: You'll need a Bible, wax paper, and old magazines.

Experience

Have kids form pairs and sit with their backs to each other. Give one partner an old magazine and the other partner a square of wax paper. Ask the partner in each pair with the magazine to find a picture of a person. Have the other partner be the "judge" and hold the wax paper

Teacher Tip
You can use a variety of translucent materials for this activity, including colored acetate, 3-D glasses, plastic bottles, and soapy eyeglasses or sunglasses. However be sure to avoid plastic wrap or plastic bags since they can cause suffocation.

up about one-half inch from his or her eyes. Then tell partners to face each other. Ask the judges each to try to describe the person in their partner's magazine while looking through the wax paper. When the judges are finished describing, let them look without the wax paper at the pictures. Then have the partners switch roles.

Response

When everyone has had a chance to be a judge, ask:

● **What was easy or difficult about describing the person in the magazine picture?**

● **What does it mean to judge?**

● **What was it like to judge someone you couldn't really see?**

● **How did the person look different when you removed the wax paper?**

Read aloud Matthew 7:1-5, and then ask:

● **Why do you think Jesus tells us not to judge others?**

● **How is judging others like describing someone while looking through wax paper?**

● **When we look at others—even without something blocking our vision—what are some things that keep us from seeing them clearly?**

● **What might be harmful about judging others?**

Say: **We're not supposed to judge other people because we can't see their hearts or lives clearly. Jesus tells us that because we all sin, we're supposed to confess our own sins instead of judging other people for their sins.**

Closing

Have kids form a circle. Begin a prayer by saying: **Dear Lord, please help us appreciate others instead of judging them.** Then say something you appreciate about the child to your left. Have kids each finish the prayer by saying something they appreciate about the person to their left.

Teacher Tip

If kids complain that they can't see the pictures very well through the wax paper, let them know that it's part of the activity. Encourage kids to describe what they do see, even if it's only fuzzy shadows or blocks of color. The questions in the Response section will help clarify the activity for kids.

Being True to Your Word

THEME: Keeping promises
SCRIPTURE: Matthew 5:33-37
OVERVIEW: Kids will design a craft that will show that saying they will do something is as important as promising to do something.
PREPARATION: You'll need a Bible. You'll also need construction paper and markers for each person.

Experience

Have kids pair up, then ask pairs to discuss the following questions. Ask:

● **Can you think of a time you made a promise and kept it? What happened?**

● **Can you think of a time you made a promise and didn't keep it? What happened?**

● **Have you ever said you would do something, then didn't? What happened?**

● **Is making a promise more important than just saying you will do something? Explain.**

Distribute construction paper and markers. Show kids how to fold the construction paper lengthwise into thirds, forming a Z fold.

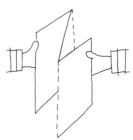

Have kids fold their papers and write their names on both sides of the folded paper. Then have kids open their papers by opening one flap. Inside the opening have kids write, "Yes, I will" and leave a blank space underneath. Next have kids refold the paper, turn it over, open the flap, and write on the inside, "I promise to" and leave a blank space underneath.

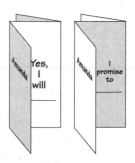

Response

Read aloud Matthew 5:33, and explain that people in Jesus' day believed that if someone promised something and used God's name, the promise was more important than if they had said something without promising.

Say: **Think about a promise you made or need to make to someone. For example, you may have promised some friends that you would play with them after school.**

Have kids choose a promise and write it on the "I promise to" side of their craft. Read aloud Matthew 5:33-37, repeating verse 37. Have kids write the same statement on the "Yes, I will" side of their craft that they wrote on the other side.

Closing

Have kids gather in a large circle with their crafts. Say: **Jesus wants you to say what you mean. If you say you're going to do something, it's just as important as if you had promised to do something.**

Have kids throw their crafts (like throwing a paper airplane) into the center of the circle. Say: **When I say "go," I want each of you to find your paper and sit down next to it, without picking it up. Go!**

Have all the kids open up their papers. Next have kids whose papers are showing "I promise to" say the statements they've written there aloud. Then have the rest of the kids read their "Yes, I will" statements aloud. Say: **You wrote a promise to do something on one side of your paper. You wrote the same thing without a promise on the other side. Remember that Jesus says that if you say you will do something, it's as important as a promise. Take your paper with you to remind you of what Jesus said.**

Close with a prayer asking Jesus to help kids to be true to their word—whether they promise or not.

One in the Spirit

THEME: Sharing your faith
SCRIPTURE: Galatians 5:22-25
OVERVIEW: Kids will learn more about sharing the fruit of the Spirit with each other as they see that we are all interconnected in faith.
PREPARATION: You'll need a Bible, newsprint, a marker, tape, and a ball of yarn. Write Galatians 5:22-25 on the newsprint before class, and post it where kids can see it.

Experience

Have kids sit in a circle, and read Galatians 5:22-25 aloud. Say: **I have a ball of yarn here. We're going to pass it around the circle as we answer several questions about the fruit of the Spirit. Each time you answer a question, I'd like you to lightly wrap the yarn around your wrist once. When you're finished, hand the yarn to the person on your right.** Begin by asking:

● **Which fruit do you demonstrate to the people around you?**

Have kids pass the yarn around the circle, with each person answering the question and wrapping the yarn around his or her wrist. Encourage kids to refer to the newsprint list of the fruits of the Spirit. Then ask:

● **Which fruit would you like to have more of to share with other people?**

Repeat the process, then ask:

● **What's one thing you could do this week to share the fruit of the Spirit with people you know?**

Response

After each person has answered the last question, say: **You'll notice that we're all connected to each other now. We're also all connected to each other in faith. One way we can strengthen our connection to each other is by using the fruit of the Spirit to encourage each other.**

Say: **Now let's go around the circle one more time. This time I'd like you to complete this sentence for the person on your right: "The fruit of the Spirit I see in your life is** (name of spiritual fruit) **because you…"**

Closing

Close with a prayer asking God to help children encourage each other.

Honest Only

THEME: Honesty
SCRIPTURE: Ephesians 4:29
OVERVIEW: Kids will examine how important it is to be honest with friends even when honesty is difficult.
PREPARATION: You'll need a Bible and a small, breakable toy.

Experience

When children have gathered, show them the small toy. Say: **Pretend this toy belongs to someone you're mad at. Maybe it's a friend who was mean to you or a brother who took something of yours. Think about who that might be. Let's call that person "friend X."**

When everyone has someone in mind, place the toy on the floor, and step on it to intentionally break it. Then gather up the pieces and ask:

● **What did you think when I broke this toy?**

● **How do you think friend X will feel?**

● **What are we going to tell friend X when he or she comes looking for this toy?**

Press kids for several possible things to tell friend X. Some answers may be truthful; others may not be. Then ask:

● **What do you think would happen to your friendship if you lied about what happened?**

● **What do you think would happen to your friendship if you told the truth about what happened?**

● **What do you think God would want you to do?**

Response

Say: **God wants us to be honest, even when it's hard.** Ask:

● **Why do you think God wants us to always be honest with our friends?**

Say: **Let's look at what the Bible says about how our honesty can affect our friendships.**

Have someone read aloud Ephesians 4:29. Then ask:

● **What is "unwholesome talk"? What are some examples of unwholesome talk?**

Have kids list as many examples as possible.

Have kids form pairs to discuss the following questions. Have volunteers report their responses to the group after each question. Ask:

- **How can dishonesty tear down a friendship?**
- **How can honesty be good for a friendship?**

After kids have reported, say: **Honesty in a friendship is important because it helps us learn that we can trust each other. And without trust, friendships will almost always fall apart.**

Closing

Have kids remain in their pairs. Say: **Now I'd like you to share with your partner one situation in which it's hard for you to be honest.**

Give kids a couple of minutes to share, then say: **Now I'm going to wrap up this devotion with prayer. As I pray, pray silently for your partner, asking God to help your partner be honest in friendships.**

Pray, asking God to help you and your kids always to be honest and seek to build friendships based on honesty.

Teacher Tip

"Unwholesome talk" is a term from the New International Version. In your question, use whatever term your translation uses.

INSTANT DEVOTIONS ABOUT Faith

Trust Me

THEME: God's promises
SCRIPTURE: John 14:1
OVERVIEW: Children will talk about ways to heal troubled hearts and relate this to trusting in Jesus.
PREPARATION: You'll need a Bible and transparent tape. Prepare a paper heart for each child and one for yourself. Then number the hearts in pairs. For example, make two ones, two twos, and so on.

Experience

Hand each child a paper heart. Say: **Find your partner by looking for another person with the same number on the heart as you have on yours. When you've found your partner, sit down together.** Give children a few minutes to find their partners.

Say: **Now that you've found your partner, listen closely to a Bible verse. I'm going to read something that Jesus said.** Read aloud John 14:1. Say: **In this verse, Jesus talks about troubled hearts. Discuss the following questions with your partner. Then if you have something you want to share with the whole group, raise your paper heart in the air, and I'll call on you.** Ask:

● **What kinds of things bother you and give you a troubled heart?**

● **What does it feel like to have a troubled heart?**

Say: **We've all had troubled hearts. Sometimes it feels as if our hearts are torn apart like this.** Tear your paper heart in two, then ask children to tear their paper hearts also.

Response

Say: **Let me read this Bible verse again.** Repeat John 14:1. Then say: **Now talk with your partner about these questions:**

● **When our hearts are troubled, who can we go to for help?**

● **How can we help our families and friends when their hearts are troubled?**

Ask children to give their heart halves to their partners. Pass out pieces of tape to children, and say: **Now I want you to tape your partner's broken heart together to show that we can trust Jesus with our troubled hearts. After you tape the heart back together, return the heart, and stand in a circle with the whole group.**

Closing

As children tape the hearts, tape your own torn heart and then join kids in a circle. Say: **This is a wonderful Bible verse! Jesus promises that we can trust him and his Word. In fact, we can trust him with our whole heart!** Hold up your taped paper heart.

Say: **Let's hold up our hearts and practice saying this Bible verse together.** Repeat John 14:1 slowly so that children can follow along. Then pray, thanking Jesus for his trustworthy words of comfort and love.

Praise Relay

THEME: Praise and worship

SCRIPTURE: Hebrews 13:15

OVERVIEW: Children will run a relay race to experience the power of praise and worship.

PREPARATION: You'll need a Bible and a large area with plenty of room to run. Before the devotion, set up a simple relay race in a large, open area. Mark a starting line and a marker, such as a folding chair, about twenty yards away.

Experience

Form two teams. Explain the rules: Each person will run to the marker, do five jumping jacks, hop back to the starting line, and exchange a high five with the next person in line. Encourage children to cheer loudly for each other as they run the race.

After the race, say: **Let's run the race again. Only this time, no one is allowed to cheer in any way. You can't make any noise, and you can't even silently cheer for each other.**

After this race, have children sit on the ground and catch their breath.

Response

Say: **Let's spend a few minutes comparing and contrasting these two races. Tell me how these two races were similar and how they were different.** Give children a few minutes to share their impressions of the game. Then ask:

● **Which game did you like more? Why?**

● **What would it be like if there was no cheering at football games or soccer matches? What would it be like if you were in the stands? What would it be like if you were one of the athletes?**

Say: **"Praise" is a word that's very similar to the word "cheer." In church we talk about praising God, and our worship times are designed to praise God. The Bible encourages us to praise God. Listen to Hebrews 13:15.** Read the verse aloud.

Say: **We don't always praise God "continually." In fact, sometimes there's a long time between praise times.** Ask:

● **Do you think God misses hearing our praise the same way we missed hearing our friends cheer for us? Why or why not?**

● **Why do you think the Bible tells us to continually praise God?**

● **What has God done that's worthy of our praise?**

Closing

Form groups of three to five, and ask groups to each create a cheer for God. Give groups three or four minutes to work on their cheers, then have the kids share their cheers with the entire group. End the devotion by offering a prayer of praise.

Tickling Trickles

THEME: Temptation
SCRIPTURE: I Corinthians 10:13; James 4:7
OVERVIEW: Children will be tempted by drops of water and develop a strategy to help them resist temptation.
PREPARATION: You'll need a Bible, a glass of water, a towel, newsprint, and a marker.

Experience

Have children sit in a circle. Ask them each to push their sleeves above their elbows and hold one arm straight above their heads. Wet your fingers in a glass of water, and put a drop of water on each child's wrist. Be sure to put enough water on children's wrists to allow the water to trickle down their arms. Tell children to endure the temptation of the tickling, trickling water—they shouldn't wipe the water away or lower their arms until you tell them to.

After you've put water on everyone's wrist, wait a minute or two until the water has trickled all the way down children's arms. Then pass a towel around, and have kids wipe off their arms.

Response

Ask:

● **Compare this experience to temptation. How is it like or unlike being tempted to do something wrong?**

● **What tempts people?**

Form two groups. Have group 1 read James 4:7 and group 2 read 1 Corinthians 10:13. Have each group discuss this question:

● **What does this Scripture teach us about how to face temptation?**

After groups have read their Scriptures and discussed the question, bring everyone back together, and have each group explain its findings to the other group. Then say: **Think back to the activity with the water and what you learned about temptation. Let's use that experience and what you learned from the Bible to develop several principles for resisting temptation.**

Write children's ideas on a large sheet of newsprint. Continue until children have thought of at least five ideas. Then have children boil down their answers to one-word or two-word phrases that are easy to remember. For example, they might come up with "Avoid temptation. Pray. Trust God. Resist devil. Flee temptation."

Closing

Pray: **God, we thank you for being with us to help us when we're tempted. We're glad that you've promised to help us find a way to escape temptation. You alone give us the strength and power we need to live lives that are pleasing to you. Thank you for your help. Amen.**

Balloon Power

THEME: The Holy Spirit
SCRIPTURE: John 14:16-17; John 16:13; Romans 8:26; Acts 1:8
OVERVIEW: Children will use balloons as visual reminders of the role of the Holy Spirit in their lives.
PREPARATION: You'll need five Bibles. Also provide large, uninflated balloons; a small funnel; and confetti. Photocopy the "Balloon Power" handout (p. 65), and cut apart the sections.

Experience

Say: **Even though the Holy Spirit is an important part of our faith, for many of us the Holy Spirit is a mystery. Let's make the Holy Spirit a little less mysterious today by seeing what Scripture teaches us about who the Holy Spirit is and what his role in our life is.**

Help children form five groups. Give each group a Bible and a section of the "Balloon Power" handout (p. 65), and give a balloon to each child. Have each group look up the Scripture printed on its section of the handout, read it, and be ready to demonstrate the balloon trick that's written on the slip. Tell children to also be ready to explain to the class what their Scripture teaches about the Holy Spirit and how their balloons illustrate the teaching.

Give children three or four minutes to work on their assignments.

Response

Starting with group 1, have each group teach the rest of the class what its Scripture taught and how to illustrate this with balloons.

When all the groups have shared, ask:

● **What do you know about the Holy Spirit that you didn't know before?**

● **How will knowing about the Holy Spirit's role help you in your life?**

Closing

Thank the Holy Spirit for being involved in our lives with this active prayer. Pray: **Holy Spirit, we thank you for being part of our lives. We thank you for guidance.** Have group 1 blow up balloons and let them go. **We thank you for living within us.** Have group 2 add a small amount of confetti to more balloons, blow them up, and tie them off. **We thank you for praying for us with**

Balloon Power

Photocopy this handout, and cut it apart.
You'll need one complete handout for every five students.

Group 1:

What Does the Holy Spirit Do?

SCRIPTURE: John 16:13

BALLOON TRICK: To show that the Holy Spirit guides us, your trick is to blow up your balloons and let them go. The air in the balloons "guides" the balloons all over the room!

Group 2:

What Does the Holy Spirit Do?

SCRIPTURE: John 14:16-17

BALLOON TRICK: To show that the Holy Spirit lives in us, your trick is to use a funnel to pour a small amount of confetti into the balloons. Then blow up your balloons and tie them off. The air and the confetti inside the balloons remind us of the Holy Spirit's presence in our lives.

Group 3:

What Does the Holy Spirit Do?

SCRIPTURE: Romans 8:26

BALLOON TRICK: To show that the Holy Spirit prays for us using words we can't understand, your balloon trick is to blow up the balloons, then gradually let the air out to make the balloons squeak.

Group 4:

What Does the Holy Spirit Do?

SCRIPTURE: Acts 1:8

BALLOON TRICK: To show that the Holy Spirit gives us power, your balloon trick is to blow up the balloons and tie them off. Then rub the balloons on your clothes and hold them to your heads so that your hair stands straight out.

Group 5:

What Does the Holy Spirit Do?

SCRIPTURE: John 14:16

BALLOON TRICK: To show that the Holy Spirit will be with us forever, your balloon trick is to blow up your balloons and tie them off. Then rub the balloons on your clothes so that the balloons stick to you like glue.

words we can't even understand. Have kids in group 3 make their balloons squeak. **We thank you for the power you give us to do God's will.** Have kids in group 4 rub their balloons on their clothes and hold them to their hair. **And we thank you for living with us forever.** Have kids in group 5 rub their balloons so that the balloons stick to their clothing. **Amen!**

Life Changes

THEME: The Bible
SCRIPTURE: 2 Timothy 3:16-17
OVERVIEW: Children will make several batches of modeling dough, then color it and talk about how God's Word can change them.
PREPARATION: You'll need a Bible and photocopies of the "Modeling Dough" recipe below. Gather salt, flour, cooking oil, alum, boiling water, mixing bowls, measuring cups and spoons, stirring spoons, and food coloring. You'll also need to recruit one adult helper for each group of five or six children.

Experience

Have kids form groups of five or six. Give each group a photocopy of the recipe below, ingredients, and supplies to make a batch of modeling dough. Be sure adults supervise each step of the process, especially the addition of the boiling water.

When kids have finished making the modeling dough, give each group a different color of food coloring. Instruct them to use the food coloring to change the color of the modeling dough.

MODELING DOUGH

INGREDIENTS:
1 cup salt
2 cups flour
3 tablespoons cooking oil
3 tablespoons alum
2 cups boiling water

INSTRUCTIONS:
Mix the salt and the flour together in a bowl. Add the cooking oil. Add the boiling water slowly, then stir and knead the mixture until it is well blended and smooth.

Response

When kids have finished adding coloring to their modeling dough, ask:

● **How did the modeling dough change when you added the food coloring?**

● **Did you need a lot of food coloring to change your batch of modeling dough?**

Read 2 Timothy 3:16-17 aloud. Say: **When you added food coloring to the modeling dough, just a few drops made a big difference!** Ask:

● **How do people change when they read and follow the Bible?**

● **Where does the power of God's Word come from?**

● **When you added food coloring to your modeling dough, you could see a difference when it changed color. How can people tell that you follow the Bible?**

● **Has God's Word changed you? If so, how?**

■■■■■■■■■■■

Teacher Tip

If you have lots of groups, you may want to instruct children in some groups to mix the food coloring to create more colors.

Closing

Give each child a piece of each color of modeling dough. Then instruct kids to use their modeling dough to form shapes that represent ways that following God's Word can change them. For example, a child may create a sculpture of a bed to represent making his bed every day; another child may form a gift she can give to a friend to encourage that person.

 bove All Else

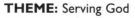

BEST for Upper-Elementary Kids

THEME: Serving God

SCRIPTURE: Daniel 3:16-18

OVERVIEW: Children will describe things that are important to them and then place the descriptions on a makeshift altar as symbols of their commitment to God.

PREPARATION: You'll need a Bible, index cards, and pencils. Be sure a table, chair, or another piece of furniture is in the room to use as an "altar."

Experience

Give each child an index card and a pencil. Instruct kids to write on their index cards a description of something that is very important to them. For example, a child might write, "basketball," "good grades," "family," or "friends."

Response

When kids have completed their descriptions, ask:

● **What are some ways you can serve God?**

● **What does it mean to give up everything to follow God?**

● **What are some examples of giving up everything to follow God?**

Say: **When the Israelites had been taken captive and were living in Babylon, Nebuchadnezzar, king of Babylon, made a tall statue and commanded everyone to bow down and worship it. Three young Israelites—Shadrach, Meshach, and Abednego—refused to worship the idol. They told the king they would worship only God. The king became very angry and told Shadrach, Meshach, and Abednego he would throw them into a blazing furnace if they didn't worship the idol.**

Read Daniel 3:16-18 aloud, then ask:

● **What impresses you about Shadrach, Meshach, and Abednego?**

● **What were Shadrach, Meshach, and Abednego committed to do?**

● **How did Shadrach, Meshach, and Abednego show their commitment?**

● **How could you show this kind of commitment to God?**

● **How do you think this kind of commitment to God would change your life? How would it affect the things that are most important to you?**

● **Where did Shadrach, Meshach, and Abednego get their strength to stand up to King Nebuchadnezzar?**

Closing

Use a table, a chair, or other furniture to set up a makeshift altar at the front of the room. Pray aloud, asking God to help you and your students to have unwavering commitment to God, then encourage kids to pray silently. When kids have finished praying, say: **Following God doesn't mean you have to give up everything else that is important to you. It does mean that your commitment to God becomes the most important thing in your life. Just as Shadrach, Meshach, and Abednego got their strength from God, God will give you the ability and desire to say no to other things when** they get in the way of your commitment to God. **If you want to, you may bring your index card to this "altar" and lay it down as a symbol of your commitment to God, showing that God is more important to you than anything else in your life.** Give kids an opportunity to place their index cards on the altar as a symbol of their commitment to God.

Indestructible Treasure

THEME: Heaven
SCRIPTURE: Matthew 6:19-21
OVERVIEW: Children will make special treasures and learn about heaven.
PREPARATION: You'll need a Bible and modeling clay.

Experience

Give each child a piece of modeling clay. Encourage children each to use the modeling clay to make a special treasure. As they work, use some modeling clay to make a treasure of your own, such as a sculpture of a favorite possession.

When kids have finished sculpting their treasures, have each person show his or her creation to the rest of the group. Proudly display what you've made—then brush it off a table or drop it so that it's squashed!

Response

After your treasure has been destroyed, ask:
- **How does it feel when a treasure is destroyed, as mine was?**
- **What are some ways treasures are destroyed?**
- **What are some treasures you've had that have been destroyed? How did you feel when that happened?**
- **How can we keep our treasures from being destroyed?**
- **Is there anything I could do to be sure this treasure I created would never be destroyed?**

Read Matthew 6:19-21 aloud.

- **What kinds of things last forever?**
- **How can we make the kind of treasures that last forever?**
- **What do you think it means to store up treasures in heaven?**

Closing

Encourage kids to name some ways they can make treasures that will last forever in heaven. Pray aloud for them to remember to focus on heaven's promise. Encourage children to take their treasures home as reminders to keep their real treasures in heaven.

Lost and Found

THEME: God's forgiveness
SCRIPTURE: Luke 15:8-10
OVERVIEW: Children will help find a treat and learn how they can become "found" through forgiveness.
PREPARATION: You'll need a Bible, a paper bag, and one foil-wrapped chocolate coin per person. Before class, hide one chocolate coin in the room.

Experience

Say: **To celebrate how wonderful we all are, let's enjoy a treat.** Pass out the chocolate coins, and tell kids to wait until everyone has a treat before eating their coins. Hand everyone but the last child a coin, and then say: **Uh-oh! I'm missing one treat! I know I had enough coins for everyone, though, so one coin must be lost somewhere in this room. Please, everyone, put your chocolate coin in this bag while we look for the lost coin.** Collect all the coins in the paper bag, and set the bag aside until later.

Encourage kids to look for the lost treat. When someone finds the treat, thank the child, ask everyone to applaud the child, and put the coin into the paper bag.

> **Teacher Tip**
> If you don't want to leave a child out, "lose" the treat for an adult volunteer instead of a child.

Response

Gather kids around you and say: **I lost a candy coin, but Jesus told a** parable about a woman who lost a real coin. A parable is a story that teaches us something. Listen carefully to the story, and try to discover what Jesus was teaching. Read aloud Luke 15:8-10, and then ask:

● How were you feeling when I said I'd lost someone's treat?

● How do you think the woman in the parable felt when she lost her coin? What did she do?

● How do we become "lost" to God as the coin was lost in the story?

Say: When we sin, we've lost our way. We've forgotten how much God loves us and wants us to do what's right. But that isn't the end of the story, is it? Ask:

● How did you feel when the lost treat was found?

● What did the woman in the parable do when she found her coin? How do you think she felt?

Say: To end the parable, Jesus said, "There is rejoicing in the presence of the angels of God over one sinner who repents." Ask:

● What does it mean to repent or to ask for forgiveness?

● If sin makes us lose our way, what do you think helps us find our way back?

● How do you think God feels when we ask him for forgiveness?

Say: When we sin, we may have lost our way. But the good news is that when we say we're sorry, God always forgives us because he loves us.

Closing

Have children pray silently, asking God's forgiveness for anything bad they've done. Close the prayer by saying: **God, thank you for always forgiving us. Amen.**

Pass out the chocolate coins, and let everyone enjoy the treat.

Untangled Lives

THEME: Sin

SCRIPTURE: Hebrews 12:1-2a

OVERVIEW: Kids will attempt to run a race while tangled up in yarn and compare that to the sins that entangle them.

PREPARATION: You'll need a Bible, a thirty-foot length of yarn for each group of four, scissors, and a basket of treats. You'll also need a sheet of paper and a pencil for each person.

Experience

This activity is best done in a large room, such as a gym, or outside in a grassy area. Form groups of four, and give each group a thirty-foot length of yarn. Space groups at least ten feet apart. Have one person in each group tie the yarn loosely around his or her leg.

Say: **I want each person to wrap the loose end of the yarn around your leg a few times and then pass the yarn to the next person in your group. Keep wrapping the yarn around your legs until it is used up. It should look like you're standing in a big spider web when you're finished.**

After kids are entangled in the yarn, have them turn away from one another so that everyone in each group is pointed in a different direction.

Say: **You're all at the starting line of a walking race. When I say "go," start walking in the direction you're facing now. Ready? Go!**

Allow kids to try to walk with their legs entangled in the web of yarn. After ten to fifteen seconds, stop the "race."

Response

Have kids sit down where they are. Ask:

● **What was it like to try to walk while you were tangled up?**

Read Hebrews 12:1-2a aloud and ask:

● **How is sin like the yarn that you are tangled up in?**
● **When have you felt that sin prevented you from reaching a goal?**
● **How can you avoid being tangled up in sin?**
● **What does it mean to "fix our eyes on Jesus"?**

Give each group a pair of scissors, and have kids carefully cut the yarn from their legs. Read Hebrews 12:2a aloud again. Give kids paper and pencils, and have them each write a sin they get tangled up in. Then have kids roll up the papers (with the writing on the inside) and tie the rolls with the pieces of cut yarn. Ask them to discuss how fixing their eyes on Jesus can help them overcome the sins they listed on their paper rolls. Give kids fresh sheets of paper, and have each one write, "I will fix my eyes on Jesus by…" Then have kids each finish the sentence with a way to prevent this sin.

Closing

Place the basket of treats at a designated finish line away from the kids. Say: **The Bible tells us to throw off the sin that entangles us. When I say "go," throw down the sin written on your paper, run to the basket of** treats, pick up a treat, and return. Go!

After kids return with their treats, say: **When we aren't tangled up in sin we can reach our goals.** Have children retrieve their papers describing how they will fix their eyes on Jesus. Have them roll up the papers and tie them with yarn as reminders to avoid the webs of sin.

Presenting...God!

THEME: Knowing God
SCRIPTURE: Ephesians 1:19-22
OVERVIEW: Kids will create commercials demonstrating God's power in the world.
PREPARATION: You'll need Bibles, poster board, and markers.

Experience

Read Ephesians 1:19-22 aloud, and say: **This passage talks about God's power in the world.** Ask:

● **What are some ways God shows his power in our world?**

Have kids form groups of four, and give each group a Bible. Say: **In your groups, I'd like you to create commercials advertising God's power. Refer back to Ephesians 1:19-22 as you work. You can choose to create either a TV commercial, a radio commercial, or a poster campaign.** Give poster board and markers to groups that choose to create poster campaigns. Give groups five minutes to complete their campaigns.

Teacher Tip

As kids are working, circulate among them and offer suggestions. Help kids focus on God's spiritual power and how God works in people's lives rather than on God's physical power.

Response

Have groups present their commercials to the class, and encourage kids to applaud each other. After the presentations, ask:

● **What are some of the ways we saw God's power portrayed in these commercials?**

● **How can knowing more about God's power and work in the world help us to know him better?**

Closing

Have students each commit to doing one thing to help them know God better during the upcoming week.

Let Go and Let God!

THEME: Trusting God
SCRIPTURE: Matthew 6:33-34
OVERVIEW: Kids will participate in a story about worry and discuss how trusting God's promises can prevent them from worrying.
PREPARATION: You'll need a Bible.

Experience

Say: **I'd like to share a story with you about a friend of mine named Jeff. Jeff was very worried. I'd like you to help me tell this story. Every time I say the words "worried" or "worry," I'd like you to make a worried face and scratch your head as you would if you were very worried. Ready? Here we go.**

One morning, Jeff woke up very early. He was very quiet at breakfast, and his mom asked, "Jeff, what's wrong? You're so quiet." Jeff said, "Mom, I'm worried (pause) **that my friend Jack won't play basketball with me today. I think he's mad at me." Then Jeff went to school. His friend Jack asked, "What's wrong, Jeff? You look worried."** Pause. **Jeff said, "I'm worried** (pause) **that our teacher might give us a test, and I haven't studied at all." Jeff went home after school, and sat at the kitchen table to do his homework. His older sister sat down next to him and said, "How are you, Jeff?" Jeff replied, "I'm worried** (pause) **that Mom and Dad might get divorced because they were fighting earlier." Jeff went to bed that night, but he couldn't sleep. He woke up his mom, and she asked, "What's wrong, Jeff?" Jeff said, "I'm worried** (pause) **that God doesn't love me."**

Response

Ask:

● **Jeff was terribly worried about a lot of things. Do you ever worry about any of the things Jeff worried about?**

74

- **What makes you feel better when you're worried?**

Read Matthew 6:33-34 aloud, and ask:

- **What does this passage tell us about worrying?**
- **How could this passage have helped Jeff?**
- **Why do you think God doesn't want us to worry?**
- **What does God want us to do instead of worrying?**

Closing

Have kids form pairs and share things they're worried about, if they feel comfortable doing so. Then have pairs close in prayer for each other, asking God to help them not to worry but instead to keep their eyes on him.

Long-Distance Provider

THEME: Prayer

SCRIPTURE: 1 John 5:14

OVERVIEW: Kids will communicate a message across a room without speaking in order to learn about prayer.

PREPARATION: You'll need Bibles.

Experience

Have kids form pairs. Have one person from each pair huddle with you while their partners wait outside of the huddle.

Whisper to the group in the huddle: **I have a message I want you to give your partner, but you won't be allowed to say the message aloud. You'll have to try to communicate it by using motions and gestures—just as if you were playing Charades. Don't try to give the message until you're instructed to do so. The message is "God hears your prayers." Does everyone know what the message is?**

Have the group that huddled with you stand against a wall. Have children who were outside of the huddle stand against the opposite wall so each person is directly across the room from his or her partner.

Say: **Your partners have a message for you. But they are going to com-municate it to you without saying a word. Now I'd like all the kids who were in the huddle with me to communicate the message to your partners without saying anything.**

Give children about two minutes to communicate their message. Encourage children who were outside of the huddle to guess the message, but don't allow their partners to say anything.

Response

Have kids get together with their partners. Make certain each pair has a Bible, then have pairs discuss the following questions:

● **What was it like to try to communicate the message to your partner without speaking? without being near to him or her?**

● **What was it like to try to receive the message?**

● **What was the message you were trying to communicate to your partner?**

● **Read 1 John 5:14 with your partner. Is praying to God more like communicating across a room without speaking or more like communicating face to face? Explain.**

Say: **We don't have to play Charades—or any other game—to communicate with God. When we pray, he hears us. Prayer is just like talking to someone face to face—only it's with God. God loves you and cares about you more than any human possibly could.**

Closing

Say: **Let's take some time to put this devotion into practice. I'd like everyone to move as far away from others as the room allows and talk with God. You can pray aloud or you can pray silently. Either way, you can be sure that God will hear your prayer.**

Give kids a couple of minutes to pray. Then pray aloud to bring the devotion to a close.

God Gave

THEME: God's love

SCRIPTURE: Romans 5:7-8

OVERVIEW: Kids will experience the difficulty of giving and will examine what Jesus gave for us.

PREPARATION: You'll need a Bible and lots of catalogs or fliers advertising things kids would like to have. You'll also need paper, scissors, glue sticks, and a basket.

Experience

Give each child a sheet of paper and a catalog or advertising flier. Have kids cut pictures of things they have now or that they'd like to have. Have each student select six or seven things and glue them to the paper.

When kids have finished, say: **Now we're going to play a little game. First, let's pretend that you own all of the items on your sheet. I'm going to describe a person, and you need to decide if you'd give up any or all of the items on your sheet for that person. If you would, tear those items from your sheet, paper and all, and place them in the basket I pass around.**

When kids understand the instructions, read one description from the following list, pause while kids decide, and pass around the basket. When the basket gets back to you, move on to the next description. Keep going until you've gone through the list.

● **a homeless six-year-old whose only possessions are the clothes he's wearing, a tattered jacket, and a worn teddy bear with an eye missing**

● **a mother who doesn't make very much money and has four children to feed and clothe**

● **a teenager whose parents kicked her out of the house**

● **a schoolmate who has about as many things as you do**

● **a boy who has everything he wants and constantly teases you because you don't have all the things he has**

When you're finished, have kids show what they have left. Then read aloud Romans 5:7-8.

Ask:

● **How did you feel when you were asked to give something to the boy who had everything and teased you?**

Read Romans 5:7-8 aloud again. Then ask:

● Is what Jesus did for us similar to what we were asked to do for the boy who had everything? Explain.

● How is it different?

Say: **Jesus loved us so much that he was willing to give his life for us, even when we were doing things he hated and not caring anything about him.**

Response

Say: **When Jesus died for us, he did it so that we could have eternal life with him in heaven. All we have to do is believe in Jesus and follow him in our lives. Right now I'd like you to think about what your response will be to what Jesus has done for you.**

Give kids some time to think, then lead them in singing "I Have Decided to Follow Jesus" or another song of commitment to a relationship with God through Christ.

Closing

Have kids form a circle and join hands. Have them repeat the following prayer after you, a phrase at a time:

Thank you, Jesus,
For dying for us on the cross.
Help us to believe in you
And follow you always.
In Jesus' name, amen.

Teacher Tip

You may want to talk with each child individually after this devotion in order to discuss kids' responses to Jesus.

Set Free!

THEME: Eternal life
SCRIPTURE: Romans 6:22-23
OVERVIEW: Kids will experience being set free and will be challenged to accept the freedom God offers in eternal life through Christ.
PREPARATION: You'll need a Bible, index cards, and pencils.

Experience

Begin by playing the following game.

Choose three children to be Freedom Finders, one to be the Hostage Holder, and the rest of the children to be Hostages. Have all the Hostages huddle in one corner of the room. Say: **All of you Hostages are tied up and being held captive by the Hostage Holder. You can't move. You must sit still unless you're touched by a Freedom Finder. Then you're set free and become a Freedom Finder yourself. That means you can touch other kids and set them free, too. The Hostage Holder is to keep the Freedom Finders from touching any of the Hostages. If the Hostage Holder touches a Freedom Finder, the Freedom Finder must sit down and become a Hostage. Freedom Finders, your job is to set all of the Hostages free.**

Allow kids to play the game at least two or three times so that kids can play different roles. Then have them sit in a circle. Ask:

● **What was it like to be a captive?**

● **What was it like to be set free?**

Have someone read aloud Romans 6:22-23. Then ask:

● **How are people like our Hostages when they sin?**

● **How is what Jesus did for us like what the Freedom Finders did for our Hostages?**

● **How is it different?**

● **What is the freedom that God offers us like?**

Say: **God did a fantastic thing for us when he made it possible for us to be set free from sin and to live in heaven forever with him. No one else could have done it, and without what God did, we'd never be able to reach heaven.**

Response

Say: **I'm going to read those Bible verses again. While I read, think about the good things you can receive because of what God did through Jesus.**

Read Romans 6:22-23 aloud again. Then ask:

● **What good things can we receive because of what God did for us through Jesus?**

● **What is eternal life?**

● **What do you think heaven will be like?**

● **What do we have to do to receive eternal life?**

Before you move on to the closing, be sure kids understand the answer to this question.

Closing

Give kids each an index card and a pencil. Say: **Now we're going to think for a minute about our relationships with Jesus. Jesus died on the cross to free us from sin and offer us eternal life with him. Write on your card something you want to do in response to what Jesus has done for *you*. I'm not going to collect these cards, but later today I'd like each of you to share with a parent or another adult what you wrote on your card.**

After kids have written on their cards, wrap up this devotion with a prayer, asking God to help children always to believe in Jesus and to trust him to give them eternal life. Remind kids to share what they've written on their cards with a parent or another adult.

What a Friend!

THEME: Jesus as friend
SCRIPTURE: John 15:12-15
OVERVIEW: Kids will create "perfect friends" and examine what a perfect friend Jesus is.
PREPARATION: You'll need Bibles, a roll of butcher paper, scissors, watercolor markers, and newsprint or chalkboard and chalk.

Experience

Form groups of three or four. Give each group a sheet of butcher paper. The paper should be as long as your children are tall. In each group, have one child lie down on the paper while another child traces around that child with a watercolor marker.

Then say: **Now we're going to create "perfect friends." On your outlined friend, write words that describe a perfect friend. For example, on an arm someone might write, "Helps carry my things when my arms are full."**

When you're sure kids understand the instructions, give everyone a marker, and have kids begin. Make sure that each child participates by writing something. Help the younger kids yourself, or encourage older kids to help them. If kids struggle with thinking of things to write, help them out with suggestions.

When it appears that kids have run out of ideas, call time, and have each group present its perfect friend. As kids read the descriptions written on their friends, keep a list on a chalkboard or newsprint. If groups repeat earlier groups' ideas, don't write them a second time.

After all groups have reported, say: **This looks like quite a friend!** Ask:

● **What would it be like to have a friend with all of these qualities?**

● **Do any of your friends always do all of these things? Explain.**

Then say: **Let's think about who might have all these qualities.**

Response

Distribute Bibles, and have someone read aloud John 15:12-15. Then say: **Jesus is our friend. He even said to his followers that he was their friend. If we're his followers, we're his friends too. And he's the best friend a person could ever have.**

Read each item on the list you just made, and have kids suggest ways Jesus could fit the qualities of a best friend. For example, if a quality is "helps carry my things," someone could say, "Jesus helps us by carrying our load of worries."

After going through the entire list, ask:

● **What kind of friend is Jesus?**

Teacher Tip

Kids may have trouble connecting some of their qualities with Jesus. If so, help them out by suggesting general principles that fit Jesus and the qualities they listed.

Closing

Read aloud John 15:12-15 again. Ask:

● **What does this passage say Jesus wants us to do in response to his friendship and love?**

If kids have trouble answering, encourage them to read the passage one more time. Then ask:

● **How can we show love to others as Jesus has shown love to us?**

After kids have answered, have them form two equal circles, one inside the other, with kids on the inside circle facing those on the outside. Each child should have a partner across from him or her. Say: **Tell the person across from you something that shows you care about him or her. For example, you might say, "You're a great friend because you always listen when I talk to you" or "I'd be glad to come over and help you rake your yard sometime."**

After about thirty seconds, have the outside circle rotate to the right one person. Then have kids repeat the activity. Have kids rotate at least once more.

Close your devotion with prayer, thanking God for the fantastic friend we have in Jesus and asking God to help us show his love to others.

A Penny Saved

THEME: New Year's Day
SCRIPTURE: 2 Corinthians 5:17
OVERVIEW: Children will clean pennies and then trade pennies in for new ones to learn that Jesus has made them new.
PREPARATION: You'll need a Bible and a bucket or large bowl containing a mixture of water and mild dish soap. Bring a clean margarine container with a lid and one tarnished penny for each student in your class. Also bring three brand-new pennies for each child in your class. It's probably a good idea to have some towels handy in case of a spill.

Experience

Give each student a tarnished penny. Ask:

● **What's the difference between the penny you have and a brand-new penny?**

● **What do you think has caused your penny to become dirty?**

● **Do you feel more like a brand-new penny or one that's been around for a while? Explain.**

● **What kinds of things make us feel as if we aren't shiny and new?**

● **How can we become like brand-new pennies?**

Say: **Let's see if these pennies can be made to look new again.**

Have kids clean their pennies in the water and dish soap solution.

Response

After a few minutes, have a volunteer read 2 Corinthians 5:17 aloud. Ask:

● **How is what we did with the pennies like what Jesus did for us? How is it different?**

● **What's the difference between trying to clean something and making it brand-new?**

Say: **You did a very good job washing your pennies. But what you did doesn't completely show what Jesus did for us. He has made us clean and**

Teacher Tip

If you're unable to find new pennies for your kids, you can clean pennies by using lemon juice and salt. Pour enough lemon juice in a plate or shallow bowl to submerge one side of each penny in the juice. Pour salt on the penny, and rub the penny in the solution using one finger. Flip the penny over, and repeat the process. Pennies that aren't excessively tarnished will come out looking brand-new.

perfect on the inside as well as the outside. I have a stack of brand-new pennies here. To get one, all you have to do is turn in your old penny.

Encourage children to exchange their pennies. Ask a volunteer to read 2 Corinthians 5:17 aloud. Then ask:

● **How is exchanging your old penny for a new penny like what Jesus did for us?**

● **How is exchanging your penny a better picture of what Jesus did than washing your penny?**

● **In what ways has Jesus made us new?**

Say: **Jesus did more than clean us up. He made us brand-new! As we start this new year, let's remember that Jesus has made us brand-new people. We aren't dirty or damaged anymore. We're holy and clean.**

■■■■■■■■■■
Teacher Tip
Children will not be able to make most of the pennies look brand-new by washing them. Seize this teachable moment by reminding your kids that it's impossible for us to cleanse ourselves from sin.

Closing

Say: **On New Year's Eve, people make noisemakers to celebrate the coming of a new year. Let's make noisemakers to celebrate the fact that Jesus has made us new.**

Give each student a clean margarine container and lid and three brand-new pennies. Instruct kids to put all four of their pennies into the margarine containers and to shut the lids. Ask children to wait to make noise with their noisemakers.

Say: **I'm going to say a prayer to thank Jesus for making us new. As soon as I say "amen," make as much noise as you can with your noisemakers to celebrate the fact that you are a new creation in Jesus.**

Pray: **God, thank you for doing more than clean us up a little. Thank you for making us brand-new through the work Jesus did on the cross. Help us to live this new year for you. In Jesus' name, amen.**

Love in Action

THEME: Valentine's Day
SCRIPTURE: 1 John 3:18
OVERVIEW: Kids will create collages of love in action and discuss how they can show love to those around them.
PREPARATION: You'll need a Bible, construction paper or poster board, old magazines, scissors, glue sticks, and small heart stickers.

Experience

Read 1 John 3:18 aloud, and ask:

● **What does it mean to love people "with actions and in truth"?**

Have kids form trios, and give each trio a piece of construction paper or poster board, some old magazines, scissors, and glue sticks. Say: **You're going to create "Love in Action" collages in your trios. I'd like you to look through your magazines and find pictures of people showing love to others. You might find a picture of a mother and child together or a picture of someone showing kindness to another person. Cut your pictures out, and glue them to your paper.**

Give trios a few minutes to create their collages, and then have trios share their collages with the whole group.

Response

Ask:

● **What are some ways you can show love to people around you?** Have each person in each trio commit to one way of showing love during the upcoming week.

Closing

Close in prayer, asking God to help children show love to those around them, then give each person a heart sticker as a reminder of his or her commitment.

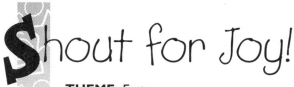

Shout for Joy!

THEME: Easter

SCRIPTURE: Matthew 28:1-10

OVERVIEW: Children will demonstrate ways to express sadness and happiness, then celebrate Jesus' resurrection.

PREPARATION: You'll need a Bible.

Experience

Say: **Think about the saddest thing that could possibly happen to you.** Ask:

● **How would you show your sadness?**

Show us what you would do if you were as sad as you could possibly be.

After kids have demonstrated the actions they've described, say: **Now think about the happiest thing that could possibly happen to you.**

Ask kids how they would show their happiness, and encourage them to demonstrate those actions.

Response

Read Matthew 28:1-10 aloud, then ask:

● **What did the women in this story discover when they went to Jesus' tomb?**

● **How do you think they felt when they were on their way to the tomb? What did they expect to find?**

● **How do you think they felt after they discovered that Jesus had come back to life?**

● **Why did their emotions change so much when they got to the tomb?**

● **How would you have felt if you had been at the tomb with the women?**

Closing

Assign children a sequence for expressing sadness then joy, using some of the ideas they came up with earlier. For example, you might tell kids to plan to cry then shout "hallelujah," frown then smile, lie down then jump up and down, and put their heads in their hands then clap their hands. On the count of three, lead children in carrying out their assigned actions in praise to God, then yelling, "Jesus is risen!" Have children repeat this process a few times.

Thanks, Mom

THEME: Mother's Day

SCRIPTURE: Proverbs 1:8-9

OVERVIEW: Children will honor their mothers by creating paper chains describing some of the things their mothers have taught them.

PREPARATION: You'll need a Bible, watercolor markers, and transparent tape or a stapler. Prepare at least twenty one-by-four-inch strips of colored paper for each child and one two-by-eight-inch strip for each child.

Experience

Give each child at least twenty paper strips. Provide several watercolor markers for kids to share. Say: **Since we're celebrating Mother's Day this week, we're going to think about our mothers today. On each slip of paper, write one thing your mother has taught you.**

If kids have trouble, spark their thinking with ideas such as how to eat, how to dress, how to turn on a faucet, how to open a door, and so on.

Teacher Tip

If children in your group are too young to write, have older children or adult helpers assist them during this activity.

After kids have completed their strips, have them make paper chains by looping each strip with another strip then taping or stapling it to create a "link." Then demonstrate how to make a chain into a necklace by looping the ends together. Have kids put their paper chains around their necks. Ask:

● **How did you feel as you thought of all those things your mother has helped you learn?**

● **How important are the things you've learned from your mother?**

Say: **The things we've learned from our mothers have helped us become who we are. God wants us to keep learning from our mothers just as we already have.**

Response

Have someone read aloud Proverbs 1:8-9. Ask:

● **How can a mother's teaching be like a garland for your head or a chain for your neck?**

● **What does the paper chain you made do for your appearance?**

● **How does your chain honor your mother?**

Teacher Tip

If some children in your group don't live with their mothers, allow them to write things their primary caregivers have helped them learn.

Closing

Have children each write on a two-by-eight-inch strip of paper a message thanking their mothers for all they have taught them. Then tell them to loop the strip around the necklace and let it hang from the chain like a pendant. Encourage kids to give the necklaces to their mothers.

Wrap up your devotion by thanking God for all that mothers teach us.

Teacher Tip

If possible, have kids' mothers join you for the end of this devotion. Have each child put the chain around his or her mother's neck and say, "Your teaching makes me a better person. Thank you."

World's Most Honored Dads

THEME: Father's Day
SCRIPTURE: Deuteronomy 5:16
OVERVIEW: Kids will make certificates of honor for their fathers.
PREPARATION: You'll need a Bible. Make one "blue ribbon" for every eight kids, and have tape on hand to attach the ribbon to children's clothing. You'll also need one photocopy of the "Certificate of Honor" (p. 91) for each child, markers, and chalkboard and chalk or newsprint.

Experience

Have kids form a circle. Choose one child to stand in the middle of the circle, and tape the ribbon you made before class on his or her chest. Then say: **Right now we're going to honor** (child's name). **Each of us will say something we like about** (child's name), **and then we'll all clap. I'll start.**

Begin by saying something such as "I really like Sandy's big smile." Then lead everyone in a round of applause. Have the person on your left go next, and continue around the circle. Have the last person to say something be the next person to stand in the middle of the circle. Continue until all the kids have been honored in the center of the circle.

Ask kids to sit down, then ask:

Teacher Tip

If there are more than twelve kids in your group, form circles of six to eight kids, with one child in the center of each circle. Be sure to help kids in all the circles get started.

● How did it feel to have others saying nice things about you?

● How did our words and actions honor the person in the center?

Say: **There are some people in our lives God wants us to honor. Let's take a look at the Bible to see who they are.**

Have someone read aloud Deuteronomy 5:16. Say: **This verse talks about both parents, but since we're celebrating Father's Day this week, we're going to talk about honoring our fathers.** Ask:

● **How is what we did in honoring each other like the way God wants us to honor our fathers?**

● **How is it different?**

Say: **Saying nice things and clapping are not the only ways to honor someone. Lets think of some other ways.**

Teacher Tip

Be sensitive to kids who may not have fathers at home. Suggest that they could give the certificates to their primary caregivers or send them to their fathers.

Response

Ask:

● **What kinds of things can we do to honor our fathers?**

As kids answer, make a list on a chalkboard or newsprint. Keep going until you have a list of at least ten positive things kids can do.

Give each person a "Certificate of Honor" (p. 91) and a marker. Have kids personalize their certificates, mentioning things their fathers do for them and also listing a couple of things from the list you just made, promising to honor their fathers in specific ways.

Teacher Tip

If children in your group are too young to write, have older children or adult helpers assist them during this devotion.

Closing

If it's possible to have fathers present, have kids give the certificates to their fathers, thanking them for all they do. If fathers can't be present, encourage kids to take the certificates to them later.

End the devotion with prayer, asking God to help kids honor their fathers in a special way during the upcoming week and in everyday ways all year long.

Certificate of Honor

# Giving Thanks

THEME: Thanksgiving
SCRIPTURE: Psalm 147:1-9
OVERVIEW: Children will find objects to represent what they're thankful for, then thank God for his gifts.
PREPARATION: You'll need a Bible. Recruit several adult helpers for this devotion, one adult for every two or three children if possible.

Experience

Have children form small groups of two or three. Assign each group an adult leader. Tell groups to search the building or the grounds for objects symbolizing things they're thankful to God for. (Each child is to find at least one object.) Children may be thankful for the actual objects they find or for something they symbolize. For example, if a child finds a leaf, he or she may use it to indicate thankfulness for leaves or thankfulness for autumn. Instruct children to bring their objects back to the meeting area within five minutes. (If you prefer, instruct children to make a list of the objects rather than bringing them back to the meeting area.)

Response

When children have returned to the meeting area, read Psalm 147:1-9 aloud, then ask:
- **What are some of the works of God this Scripture passage mentions?**
- **What objects did you find to show us?**

Have children show the group what they found and describe why they're thankful for these things. Then ask:
- **What is the Thanksgiving holiday for?**
- **Why do you think we have a whole holiday about thanking God?**

Closing

Have children form a circle and put all their objects in the middle of the circle. Then have kids take turns offering sentence prayers thanking God for the blessings he provides.

Promises, Promises

THEME: Christmas
SCRIPTURE: Isaiah 8:22–9:2, 6-7; John 1:1-5
OVERVIEW: Children will see that Christmas is a time to celebrate the fulfilled prophecies of God's Word.
PREPARATION: You'll need a Bible, pennies, pencil, paper, and Christmas lights.

Experience

Have children form pairs. Give each pair a penny, a sheet of paper, and a pencil. Say: **With your partner, decide who will be the Tosser and who will be the Recorder. Give the Tosser the penny, and give the Recorder the pencil and paper.** Give children a moment to carry out these instructions.

Say: **The Tosser will toss the penny ten times, and the Recorder will write down how many times the penny lands heads up and how many times the penny lands tails up. But before you start tossing, I want both partners to predict how many times it will land heads up and how many times it will land tails up. Write down your predictions, then start tossing.**

Give children a couple of minutes to make predictions and toss the pennies. Then have children compare their results with their predictions. Find out how many children were exactly right in their predictions, how many were off by one or two, and how many were off by several.

Gather the pennies, paper, and pencils. Then say: **When you toss pennies, it's not too hard to make predictions because there are a limited number of possible outcomes. A penny can either land heads up or tails up—those are the only two possibilities. But still, very few of us can accurately predict what will happen when we toss a penny ten times. Think how much harder it would be to accurately predict the future!**

Let's spend a few minutes predicting what will happen in the future. Talk with your partner about what you think life will be like five hundred years from now. Talk about schools, homes, and transportation.

Give children a few minutes to talk. Then have volunteers share their ideas. Ask:

- **What was hard about predicting the future?**
- **What was easy about predicting the future?**
- **Do you think people five hundred years ago—in the 1500s—could have predicted what our life is like now? Why or why not?**

Response

Say: **In biblical times there were certain men who were called to be prophets. God gave them special messages to tell to the people, and some of those messages were predictions about the future. Isaiah was one of God's prophets. Listen to these verses from the book of Isaiah. I want you to listen for two things. First listen for the problem. Then listen for the solution.**

Read aloud Isaiah 8:22–9:2, 6-7. Ask:

- **What was the problem?**
- **What do you think caused the problem?**
- **What was the solution?**
- **Why do you think Isaiah calls Jesus the light?**

Say: **Isaiah wrote this prophecy seven hundred years before Jesus was born. The Jews looked forward to Jesus' birth for hundreds and hundreds of years.**

- **How do you think the Jews felt when they realized that Jesus was the one Isaiah had promised?**
- **Not everyone believed that Jesus was the promised one. What reasons can you think of that might explain why they didn't believe?**

Say: **We know that everything in God's Word is true. Isaiah prophesied that Jesus would come and that he would be a light to the world. Listen to what the Gospel of John has to say about Jesus.**

Read aloud John 1:1-5. Then say: **Let's decorate our room to celebrate Jesus, the light of the world.**

Closing

Have children decorate the room with Christmas lights. Darken the room, light the Christmas lights, and pray: **Jesus, long ago the prophet Isaiah promised that you would come and that you would be the light of the world. On Christmas we celebrate the promise that came true. You came to our world as a light in the darkness. Jesus, we celebrate your birth. Thank you for coming. Amen.**

Happy Birthday!

BEST for Upper-Elementary Kids

THEME: Christmas
SCRIPTURE: Luke 2:1-7
OVERVIEW: Children will plan a birthday party and then carry out their plans to celebrate Jesus' birth.
PREPARATION: You'll need a Bible, a marker, newsprint, and other supplies as kids determine during the activity.

Experience

Ask kids what they would plan if they were going to plan a birthday party. As children call out ideas, write their ideas on a sheet of newsprint. For example, kids may list birthday cake, paper hats, decorations, gifts, and entertainment.

Response

Read Luke 2:1-7 aloud, and say: **The Bible verses I just read describe Jesus' birthday—the day God was born as a human so he could live with us, show us how to love him, and die to save us from our sins. This is a reason for celebrating the ultimate birthday!**

Instruct children to go through the list of party-planning ideas and "translate" them into ways they can celebrate Jesus' birthday. For example, if kids listed birthday cake, they might "translate" that into sharing the Lord's Supper or providing food for needy people. Paper hats might be changed to wearing special festive attire or providing clothing for needy people. Decorations may become a Christmas tree or enjoyment of the beauty of God's creation. Gifts may be translated to giving Christmas gifts to others or sharing gifts such as obedience, love, and encouragement. Entertainment may become singing hymns of praise or encouraging others with Christmas caroling.

Closing

Help students plan an actual birthday party for Jesus. The party can last as long as a few minutes or several weeks. Help kids come up with a specific plan for carrying out their celebration. Then help kids form committees to carry out the specifics of their plan.

Scripture Index